A Quick English Reference

J.S. HOOPER

KUALA LUMPUR
OXFORD UNIVERSITY PRESS
TOKYO SINGAPORE HONG KONG
1980

Preface

The main purpose of *A Quick English Reference* is to provide help and guidance for intermediate students of English as a second or foreign language who need a reference book of useful items to supplement the English taught in schools. It also provides the layman with a quick reference on a variety of aspects of English.

The book is organized into five parts: The Syntax of English, The Mechanics of English, Expression in English, Vocabulary Building in English, and Units of Writing.

Part 1, The Syntax of English, supplies essential information about the grammatical forms and structures of all the major and minor word classes. Part 2, The Mechanics of English, provides students with useful information and handy tips on punctuation and spelling. Part 3, Expression in English, aims to help students overcome problems with one of the more difficult aspects of the language—its idiomatic usage. Useful words for expressing numerous concepts and ideas in English, as well as the more traditional aspects of English vocabulary such as derivations and antonyms and synonyms, are presented in Part 4, Vocabulary Building in English. The final part, Units of Writing, gives summaries of the main types of letters students are expected to write in English.

A Quick English Reference is a useful reference book for both English language students and adults who need English in their everyday lives.

J. S. HOOPER
October 1980

Contents

v

PART

The Syntax of English

1 Introductory Definitions

In order to build a sentence, you must first understand some basic facts about sentences.

1. The Meaning or Function of Sentences

There are several kinds of sentences. These can be classified according to the way they are used:

A. A *declarative* sentence makes a statement of fact or a statement of opinion. In it the subject usually comes before the verb:

> The door is open.

B. An *imperative* sentence gives a command or makes a request:

> John, close the door.
> Will you close the door, John.

C. An *interrogative* sentence asks a direct question. The sentence begins with an interrogative word:

> What shall we have for lunch?

D. An *exclamatory* sentence shows strong or sudden feeling. Such sentences usually begin with **what** or **how** and end with an exclamation mark:

> What a nuisance!
> How did I make that mistake!

Whatever its function, every sentence has a subject and a predicate. In the imperative sentence the subject is understood to be 'you'. The remaining elements that make up sentences are either modifiers or complements.

2

2. Sentence Structure

A. *Subjects*. The subject of a sentence is the person or thing the subject is about. In some sentences the subject is understood, e.g. Stop! (the subject 'you' is understood). Generally though, the complete subject includes the noun or noun substitute alone, without any of its modifiers. It normally occurs before the verb in sentences: e.g.

> The *woman* in the frilly pink dress came into the room.
> (the noun 'woman' is the subject)
> Where are *you* going?
> (the noun substitute, pronoun 'you', is the subject)

A **compound subject** consists of two or more nouns or noun phrases:

> *Anne* and *Peter Eden* are playing badminton with us tonight.

B. *Predicates*. The predicate of a sentence consists of the verb and its modifiers and complements. The predicate expresses the action or condition of the subject. Predicates may be simple or compound:

The **simple predicate** is the main verb or verb phrase in the predicate:

> Sue *visited* Switzerland last year. (= main verb)
> The children *were swimming* in the sea. (= verb phrase)

A **compound predicate** has two or more main verbs:

> The clown *joked*, *danced* and *sang*. (= 3 main verbs)
> He *should have bought more fish*. (= verb + complement)
> Little girls *cry very easily*. (= verb + modifier)

C. *Complements*. While some verbs are complete in themselves (The girls *ran*; Birds *fly*), other verbs need a noun, noun substitute or adjective to complete their meaning. The term complement, then, means something that is needed to complete a grammatical construction. Complements may be a direct object, an object complement, a predicative adjective, or a predicative nominative:

The **direct object** is the noun which indicates the receiver of the action:

> My brother plays the *organ*.
> She celebrated her *birthday* yesterday.

The **object complement** follows the direct object and refers to the same thing, usually after verbs of naming or calling:

> The director appointed Miss Fry a personnel *officer*.

3

The **predicative adjective** is an adjective in the predicate referring to the subject:

> Eddie Howe was *cheerful*.
> My father is quite *fat*.

The **predicative nominative** is a noun or noun subject in the predicate naming or referring to the subject:

> Those women are *dentists*.
> All of my sons have been *scouts*.

3. Modifiers

Adverbs and adjectives (and phrases or clauses acting as adverbs and adjectives, e.g. prepositional phrases), are modifiers. They limit, describe, or identify the words they modify. Thus they are used to make ideas more exact and clear. Compare:

1. He threw a stone. The *naughty* boy threw a *sharp* stone.	Adjectives modify nouns.
2. My brother repaired the radio. My brother *carefully* repaired the radio.	An adverb modifies a verb.
3. Eight a.m. is a busy time. Eight a.m. is an *unusually* busy time.	An adverb modifies an adjective.
4. The girl plays the guitar. The girl *in the red dress* plays the guitar.	A prepositional phrase modifies a noun.

4. Phrases

Phrases are groups of words which do not express a complete thought, but which act as a unit. They may function as nouns, modifiers, or verbs:

Swimming and running are two excellent forms of exercise.	A verb phrase functions as a noun.
He sat *near the pool*.	A prepositional phrase functions as an adverb.

A. A *noun phrase* is a phrase which can be the subject, object, or complement of a clause, or as a prepositional complement. A noun phrase usually has a noun as its head (i.e. main part of the phrase), although pronouns and adjectives may also be heads of noun phrases. The headword may appear together with determiners, in particular (see page 67), and one or more modifiers (see pages 42 and 49):

4

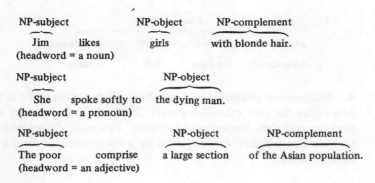

NP-subject   NP-object   NP-complement

Jim   likes   girls   with blonde hair.
(headword = a noun)

NP-subject   NP-object

She   spoke softly to   the dying man.
(headword = a pronoun)

NP-subject   NP-object   NP-complement

The poor   comprise   a large section   of the Asian population.
(headword = an adjective)

(NP = Noun Phrase)

B. A *verb phrase* consists of either a main verb (see page 22), or a main verb plus one or more auxiliary verbs (see page 54):

> My sister *reads* two story books every week.
> (Verb phrase = main verb)
> My sister *is reading* a story book about animals.
> (Verb phrase = main verb + auxiliary)

C. A *prepositional phrase* consists of a preposition (see page 85) followed by a prepositional complement—either a noun phrase, a *wh-*clause, or an *-ing* clause:

> There were 200 students in the lecture hall.
>   preposition + noun phrase
> We were not sure of what the teacher said.
>   preposition + *wh-* clause
> She brightened the house by putting fresh flowers in every room.
>   preposition + *-ing* clause

(See page 142 for examples of idiomatic prepositional phrases.)

5. Clauses

Clauses are groups of words containing both subject and predicate (i.e. a subject + verb + complement + (optional) adverbial). Almost all sentences contain at least one clause.

Thus, a typical clause structure looks like these diagrams:

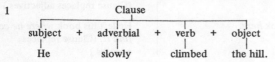

1

Clause

subject + adverbial + verb + object

He   slowly   climbed   the hill.

5

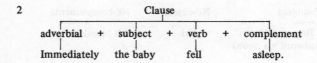

adverbial	+	subject	+	verb	+	complement
Immediately		the baby		fell		asleep.

A. *Independent (Main) Clauses* are those which are complete in themselves (like the two examples above). They can thus stand by themselves as complete sentences. Alternately, two main clauses which are equal in construction, can be joined by a conjunction to form a complete sentence:

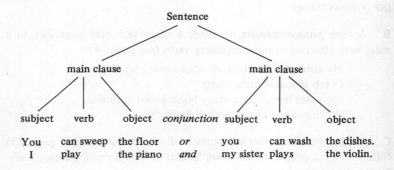

	Sentence					
main clause				main clause		
subject	verb	object	*conjunction*	subject	verb	object
You	can sweep	the floor	*or*	you	can wash	the dishes.
I	play	the piano	*and*	my sister	plays	the violin.

B. *Dependent (Subordinate) Clauses* are generally not able to stand alone as the main clause of a sentence. Usually they are included as subclauses in a main clause. As such, they act as modifiers to alter, limit, or to clarify the ideas in the main clause. They can function as nouns, adjectives or adverbs and they are normally linked to the main clause by linking words such as **that** and *wh-* words like **which** and **where**. Compare:

Independent (Main) Clauses	*Dependent (Subordinate) Clauses*
1. I realize *it*.	I realize *that he is the youngest child*. (Clause replaces a noun or pronoun.)
2. My friends went on *a round-the-world trip*.	My friends went on a trip *which took them around the world*. (Clause replaces adjectives.)
3. He left his book *here*.	He left his book *where he could find it*. (Clause replaces adverbs.)

6

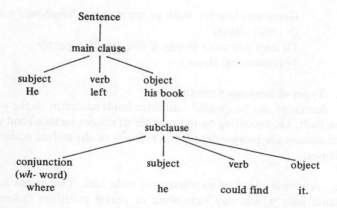

DIAGRAM OF A MAIN CLAUSE AND A SUBORDINATE CLAUSE

C. *Functions of Clauses*

1. *Relative Clauses* (introduced by *wh-* pronouns, or *that*):

   The couple, *who live next door to us*, have no children.

2. *Comparative Clauses* (introduced by *than*):

   I liked this film better *than the one we saw last week*.

3. *Nominal Clauses*:

   We are pleased *that you got the job*.
   (= *that-* clause)
   I wasn't sure *what I had to do*.
   (= *wh-* interrogative subordinate clause)
   She wants everyone *to stay the night at her house*.
   (= *to-* infinitive clause)
   Her children were busy *playing with marbles*.
   (= *-ing* clause)

D. *Adverbial Clauses*

   His son wrote to him *whenever he wanted some money*.
   (= time clause)
   They left the bag *where they had found it*.
   (= place clause)
   He fell into the drain *because he wasn't looking where he was walking*. (= reason clause)
   She wrote home *so that her mother would know she was coming*. (= purpose clause)

7

Gerry was late for work *so the manager telephoned his house.*
(= result clause)
I'll lend you some money *if you need it urgently*.
(= conditional clause)

6. Types of Sentence Structure

Sentences can be divided into three kinds according to the way they are built, i.e. according to the number of clauses included and whether the clauses are independent (main) clauses or dependent (subordinate) clauses.

A. A *simple sentence* expresses one main idea. Thus it has one main clause only which may have word or phrase modifiers (adjectives or adverbs or prepositional phrases):

My mother was born in India.

B. A *compound sentence* expresses two or more main ideas in two or more independent (main) clauses:

main idea (1)   main idea (2)

My mother was born in India but she came to Malaysia as a small girl.

C. A *complex sentence* expresses one main idea and at least one subordinate (less important) idea. Thus it contains one independent (main) clause and one or more dependent (subordinate) clauses:

main idea   subordinate idea

My mother came here from India when she was a small girl.

NOTE: Other grammatical terms used in this book will be defined as we come to them.

2 Recognizing Word Classes (or Parts of Speech)

In English it is usual to classify words into word classes (or Parts of Speech as they are more commonly known), but at the same time it is important to remember that it is the **function** of a word in a sentence which determines what part of speech a word is. For example, a word may belong to almost any word class without changing its form:

He will *fast* during the month of Ramadan. (= verb)
After one month he broke his *fast*. (= noun)
She types *fast*. (= adverb)
Marion is a *fast* worker. (= adjective)

Thus, it is necessary to consider a word in the light of the work it does in a sentence before classifying it into a particular word class.

We can distinguish between major and minor word classes:

1. Major Word Classes

1	Nouns	Singapore, city, thunder, group, honesty
2	Main Verbs	call, try, help, go, like
3	Adjectives	pretty, new, small, square, long
4	Adverbs	quickly, lively, completely, very, really

2. Minor Word Classes

1	Auxiliary Verbs	can, may, should, will
2	Determiners	a(n), the, this, every, such
3	Pronouns	I, which, mine, one, everyone
4	Prepositions	above, at, on, from, without,
5	Conjunctions	and, but, or, since, neither . . . nor
6	Interjections	oh, phew, ouch, ugh, wow

The minor word classes differ from the major word classes in that they contain a **fixed number of words**; that is, the words in these classes do not change, nor do they increase in number. In contrast, the number of words in the major word classes is always growing as people coin new words to meet new situations: e.g. atomic bomb, atomic energy, atomic number, atomic pile, atomic weight; monophonic, monorail, monomania; overcharge, overcrop, overdress.

3 Forms and Functions of the Word Classes (Parts of Speech)

Major Word Classes

1. Nouns

A. *Kinds of Nouns*

Nouns are simply 'naming words'—the words we use to refer to objects. A noun can be easily identified because it is usually modified by **a, an,** or **the.**

Nouns may be broadly classified as follows:

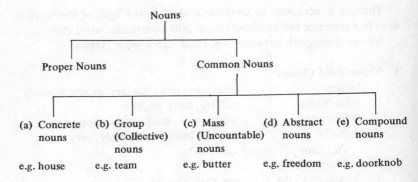

Thus, there are two main classes of nouns: Proper and Common. **Proper Nouns** refer to particular persons, places or things: Singapore, March, Mr Jones. Proper nouns are always capitalized.

Common Nouns refer to any of a class or group of persons, places, or things: city, girl, month, book, pencil. The word 'common' really means 'shared by all'. All nouns that are not Proper are Common.

(a) *Concrete Nouns* refer to objects and substances that exist in a physical sense; that is, anything that can be seen, heard, tasted, smelled, or felt by the body: bird, house, apple, child. Concrete nouns can be used with the articles (the, a, an), with numerals, and in the plural, as they are countable nouns.

(b) *Group (collective) nouns* refer to a number, or a set of persons, things, or animals regarded as a single group of the same kind: swarm, crowd, team, class, committee, group. Because they are countable they may be singular or plural: a group of teenagers, two groups of teenagers.

Special group names are used with both animate (living) and inanimate (non-living) things:

Animate

an army (of soldiers)	a gang (of thieves, labourers)
a band (of musicians)	a herd (of buffaloes, cattle)
a board (of directors)	a swarm (of bees, insects)
a crew (of sailors)	a team (of oxen, players)
a flock (of birds, sheep)	a troop (of lions, monkeys)

Inanimate

a bouquet (of flowers)	a fleet (of cars, ships)
a bunch (of grapes)	a pack (of cards)
a bundle (of rags)	a set (of clubs, tools)
a chest (of drawers)	a string (of beads)
a clump (of trees)	a tuft (of grass)

Some group nouns refer to a group of people which are related or linked in some way to each other: family, team, committee, administration, audience, class, etc. With such nouns there is a choice as to whether to use singular or plural verbs and pronouns, depending on whether they refer to individuals which make up the group or to the group as a unit:

> The family *has* brought *its* gift.
> The family *have* brought *their* gift.

> The team *is* winning the match at the moment.
> The team *are* going to celebrate if *they* win.

> The audience *is* enjoying the concert.
> The audience *are* stamping *their* feet.

(See page 14)

(c) *Mass (Uncountable) Nouns* usually refer to substances (liquid or solid) which are not normally divisible: milk, butter, sugar, oil, water, iron, glass, wood, meat, fish. Such nouns are not normally used in the plural (and, therefore, not with numerals):

> There's some tea in the cupboard.
> There are two packets of tea in the cupboard.

Mass, or uncountable, nouns may be used with determiners (in this case, group nouns) to indicate quantity and measurement, weight, etc. or other divisional terms:

Quantity: the whole cake
a segment of the cake
half of the cake
a piece of the cake
a slice of bread
a loaf of bread
two-thirds of the milk

Area: an acre of land

Length: three metres of cloth
a yard of material

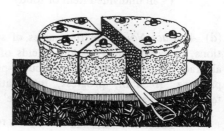

a cake

11

Weight: two kilogrammes of flour
a pound of butter
an ounce of tobacco
a ton of soil

Volume: half a litre of milk
a pint of beer
a gallon of petrol

Types/ Pine is *a type of* wood.
Species: The Toyota is *a make of* car.
Carlsberg is *a brand of* beer.
The Rajah Brooke is *a species of* butterfly.

Although some group nouns go together with particular mass nouns (e.g. a <u>tuft of grass</u>, a <u>speck of dust</u>), some group nouns can be used without such group terms: *Grasbüschel*   *Häubchen*

Bread is made of flour.

Some nouns belong to both the 'countable' and 'uncountable' classes depending on the context of the sentence:

How many *times* have you been absent this week?
(= countable)
How much *time* did you spend on your homework?
(= uncountable)

Our house is next door to some *woods*.
Most houses in rural Asia are made of *wood*.

Today I baked *a cake*.
Would you like some *cake*?

There were many *chickens* in the yard.
(= individual birds)
They eat *chicken* very often.
(= an undivided item of food)

(d) *Abstract Nouns* are the names of special qualities, actions, emotions, or conditions (including fields of study and sports). Although abstract nouns tend to be mass nouns—poverty, honesty, love, courage, patience, freedom, progress, information, democracy, philosophy, tennis—they can also be both 'countable' and 'mass' nouns:

<u>Spare</u> *a thought* <u>for</u> those poor refugees.
He was <u>deep in *thought*</u>.

12

There's *a sound* in the roof.
The Concorde can fly faster than *sound*.

The pianist played <u>*two works*</u> by Beethoven.
I have <u>plenty of *work*</u> to do this week-end.

Abstract nouns can also be used with group nouns to indicate quantity, quality, measurement and species or type:

Quantity and Quality:	an <u>item of news</u>	a <u>burst of applause</u>
	a <u>bit of advice</u>	a <u>piece of research</u>
	a <u>word of warning</u>	a <u>fit of anger</u>
Measurement:	six <u>months of hard labour</u>	
	two <u>weeks of study leave</u>	
Type/Species:	a <u>type of work</u>	
	a <u>kind of humour</u>	

(e) *Compound Nouns* consist of two or more words put together to form a name. They can be hyphenated or written separately, but they mean one thing: post office, living-room, brother-in-law, textbook, <u>doorknob</u>, check-up, grown-up.

B. *Functions of Nouns*

Function	Examples	Position
1. as subject of verb	*Alf* loves Leila.	before the verb after the verb
2. as object of verb		after the verb
(a) direct object	*Alf* loves *Leila*.	
(b) indirect object (after verbs like *buy, bring, give, take, owe, sell, write, pay*)	Alf sent *Leila* flowers.	
3. as object of preposition (in a prepositional phrase)	She took them from *Alf*.	after a preposition
4. as <u>complement</u>		after the verb
(a) subjective complement (after verbs like *be, seem, appear, become*)	Leila is the *secretary*.	

13

Function	Examples	Position
(b) objective complement (after verbs like *appoint*, *consider*, *name*, *nominate*, *choose*)	They elected Leila *secretary*.	
5. as noun adjunct	Alf waited at the *bus-stop*.	before a noun after a noun
6. as appositive	Alf, *chairman* of the committee, gave a speech.	after a noun
7. in direct address	*Alf*, come here.	usually at the beginning of a sentence

C. *Nouns and Number*

In English, nouns can have either **singular** ('one') or **plural** ('more than one') number. Singular nouns comprise:

1. Those denoting 'one': a shoe, this flower, that magazine.
2. Mass (uncountable) nouns: the tea, our democracy, that advertisement.
3. Proper nouns: Jonathan, Germany.

Usually plural count nouns (denoting 'more than one') are the only nouns which occur in the plural: two flowers, those shoes, these chopsticks.

Generally the plural is formed by adding *-s* or *-es* to the singular (see Rules on page 16) but there are two exceptions:

(i) some nouns ending in *-s* are actually singular and not plural
(ii) some nouns only ever occur in the plural

(a) *Singular nouns ending in -s*

1. Diseases: *mumps, measles, rickets*

   Measles is a common illness among young children.

2. Subject names ending in *-ics*: *statistics, linguistics, mathematics*

   Linguistics is the study of language.

3. Some games: *chess, darts, billiards, dominoes*

   Draughts is a popular game in many countries.

4. *News*

   The *news is* at nine o'clock.

14

(b) *Nouns occurring only in the plural*

1. Animals and fish: *cattle, sheep, deer, trout, salmon*

   There *are* various species of *deer* all over the world.

2. People: *people, police*

   The *police were* setting up a road-block.

3. Tools, instruments: *tongs, scissors, pliers, scales, binoculars, tweezers*
   Note: These words can be turned into ordinary count nouns by using *a pair of*.

   He used *tongs* to turn over the meat on the grill.

   She *has a pair of scissors* which she uses to cut material.

4. Articles of clothing: *trousers, spectacles, jeans, pyjamas, tights*

   His *jeans were* so tight that they split.

5. Depending on the context, a noun may occur in the plural although it may have a singular form:
   arms (weapons),
   outskirts, spirits, headquarters, stairs, surroundings

   The Russians *are* building up *their arms*.
   There *is an arms* factory near their hometown.
   There *aren't* any *funds* to build a swimming-pool.
   After his death, a scholarship fund *was* set up.

6. Some nouns have two plurals with different meanings:
   brother:

   brothers (sons of the same mother)
   brethren (members of a community)

   cloth:

   cloths (pieces of cloth)
   clothes (articles of dress)

   fish:

   fish (referring to a type/species of fishes)
   fishes (referring to individual creatures)

   shot:

   shot (non-explosive metal balls for guns)
   shots (number of actions)

   penny:

   pennies (number of coins)
   pence (amount in value)

   index:

   indexes (tables of contents to books)
   indices (signs used in mathematics)

15

We begin with a *fox*, whose plural is *foxes*,
But the plural of *ox*, is *oxen*, not *oxes*.
You may see a lone *mouse*, or a whole nest of *mice*,
But more than one *house* is *houses*, not *hice*.
If I speak of a *foot*, and two are called *feet*,
And you show me your *boot*, would a pair be called *beet*?
I may have a *brother*, or I may have *brethren*,
But though I've a *mother*, no one has *methren*.
So English, I fancy you all will agree,
Is the funniest language you ever did see.

(c) *Rules for Forming Plural Nouns*

Rule 1: Nouns are regularly made plural by the addition of -*s*:

day days, roof roofs, shoe shoes

Rule 2: Other nouns are made plural by adding -*es*:

1. Nouns ending in sibilant ('s') sounds spelled with *s, ch, sh* and *x*:

bus buses, box boxes, church churches, dish dishes

2. Nouns ending in *y* preceded by a consonant: *y* is changed to *i* (*s* only is added if *y* is preceded by a vowel):

curry curries, baby babies, key keys, monkey monkeys

3. One-syllable nouns ending in a single *f* or *fe*: *f* is changed to *v*: Exceptions: chiefs, handkerchiefs, roofs, safes, beliefs.

leaf leaves, thief thieves, knife knives

4. Nouns ending in *o*:
   -*es* only:

buffalo buffaloes, mango mangoes

   -*s* only:

bamboo bamboos, radio radios, piano pianos

Rule 3: Other nouns have other types of plural:
1. -*en* ending

children, oxen

16

2. internal vowel change	tooth teeth, foot feet, man men, woman women, mouse mice, goose geese

Rule 4: The plural of compounds:

1. In most compounds the ending *-s* is added to the last part:	boyfriends, breakdowns, grown-ups, check-ups, assistant directors, stepfathers, doorbells
2. With a few compounds, the pluralization occurs to the first part:	brothers-in-law, hangers-on, passers-by, commanders-in-chief
3. Sometimes internal vowel changes occur:	Englishmen, policemen
4. A few compounds have both the first and the last part in the plural:	menservants, women doctors

Rule 5: Foreign plurals:
There are two ways of pluralizing foreign words that have become part of the English language:
1. by the addition of the regular *-s* plural
2. by the addition of a foreign plural (usually in technical writing).
Some foreign words take both the regular and the foreign plural.

Singular Ending	Foreign Plural Ending	Regular Plural Ending	Both Plural Endings
-us	*-i*	*-uses*	*-i/-uses*
stimulus	stimuli		
bonus		bonuses	
campus		campuses	
chorus		choruses	
circus		circuses	
virus		viruses	
cactus			cacti/cactuses
focus			foci/focuses
nucleus			nuclei/ nucleuses
radius			radii/radiuses
syllabus			syllabi/ syllabuses
terminus			termini/ terminuses

17

Singular Ending	Foreign Plural Ending	Regular Plural Ending	Both Plural Endings
-a	*-ae*	*-s*	*-as/-ae*
larva	larvae		
vertebra	vertebrae		
area		areas	
dilemma		dilemmas	
diploma		diplomas	
drama		dramas	
antenna			antennas/ antennae
formula			formulas/ formulae
-um	*-a*	*-s*	*-a/-s*
curriculum	curricula		
album		albums	
museum		museums	
stadium		stadiums	
forum		forums	
memorandum			memoranda/ memorandums
aquarium			aquaria/aquariu...
symposium			symposia/ symposiums
medium			media/mediums
-ex, -ix	*-ices*	*-es*	*-ices/-es*
index	indices		
matrix			matrices/ matrixes
appendix			appendices/ appendixes
-is	*-es*		
basis	bases		
analysis	analyses		
crisis	crises		
thesis	theses		
diagnosis	diagnoses		
hypothesis	hypotheses		
-on	*-a*	*-s*	*-a/-as*
criterion	criteria		
phenomenon	phenomena		
demon		demons	
electron		electrons	
neutron		neutrons	
automaton			automata/ automatas

Singular Ending	Foreign Plural Ending	Regular Plural Ending	Both Plural Endings
-eau	-eaux	-s	-eaux/-s
bureau	bureaux		
plateau			plateaux/ plateaus

D. *Nouns and Gender*

Every noun in English belongs to one of four genders: masculine, feminine, neuter and common:

The **masculine** gender is used when the noun refers to males (persons and animals):

> man, bull, master, poet (and is used with third person pronouns *he*, *him*, *his*, etc.)

The **feminine** gender is used when the noun refers to females (persons or animals):

> woman, cow, mistress, poetess (and is used with *she*, *her*, etc.)

The **neuter** gender refers to nouns that are neither masculine nor feminine; that is, they are inanimate:

> book, water, table, happiness, democracy, biology (and is used with *it*, *its*, etc.)

The **common** gender refers to nouns that are of either sex, masculine or feminine:

> baby, person, parent, bird

Note these exceptions:

1. *He* and *she* can be used for animals whom we consider as having human qualities, especially family pets:

> Has *Blackie* had *her* milk yet?

Conversely, babies and very young children are often referred to as *it*:   *umgekehrt*

> The baby is crying for *its* milk.

2. *She* is occasionally used for inanimate objects when we consider them to have animate qualities, for example, ships and cars, and sometimes countries:

> What a beautiful yacht! What have you named *her*?
> Malaysia is celebrating *her* national day next month.

19

The **feminine gender** is shown in three ways in nouns:

    (i) by the suffix *-ess*, e.g. mistress, hostess

    (ii) by a word in front of another word,
       e.g. billy-goat → nanny-goat

    (iii) by a totally different word, e.g. nephew → niece.

Below are lists of nouns and their various genders:

Persons: Masculine and Feminine Gender:

Feminine ending in *-ess*		Other feminine endings	
Masculine	*Feminine*	*Masculine*	*Feminine*
actor	actress	bachelor	spinster
author	authoress	barman	barmaid
conductor	conductress	boy	girl
count	countess	bridegroom	bride
duke	duchess	brother	sister
emperor	empress	father	mother
god	goddess	fiancé	fiancée
headmaster	headmistress	gentleman	lady
heir	heiress	grandfather	grandmother
host	hostess	hero	heroine
manager	manageress	husband	wife
master	mistress	king	queen
mayor	mayoress	landlord	landlady
millionaire	millionairess	lord	lady
murderer	murderess	male	female
poet	poetess	man	woman
postmaster	postmistress	manservant	maidservant
prince	princess	monk	nun
proprietor	proprietress	nephew	niece
waiter	waitress	salesman	saleswoman/salesgirl
		son	daughter
		Sultan	Sultana
		uncle	aunt
		widower	widow

Persons: Common Gender

adult	companion	infant	owner	singer
ancestor	cousin	judge	parent	student
baby	doctor	juvenile	passenger	teacher
Buddhist	European	lawyer	principal	teenager
child	friend	lecturer	pupil	tourist
Chinese	guardian	Minister	relation	traveller
citizen	guest	orphan	relative	worker

20

Animals: Masculine and Feminine Gender

Feminine ending in *-ess*		Other Feminine endings	
Masculine	*Feminine*	*Masculine*	*Feminine*
lion	lioness	billy-goat	nanny-goat
tiger	tigress	boar (pig)	sow
		buck (deer/rabbit)	doe
		bull	cow
		bullock *Ochse*	heifer *Färse, ju. Kuh*
		cock (rooster)	hen
		colt	filly
		dog	bitch *Hündin*
		drake *Enterich / Erpel*	duck
		gander *Gänserich*	goose
		he-goat	she-goat
	rooster	peacock	peahen *Pfauhenne*
hen		ram (sheep)	ewe
		stallion *Hengst* (horse)	mare *Stute*
		steer *Ochse*	heifer *Färse*
		tom-cat	tabby-cat *weibliche Katze*

Animals: Common Gender *Geflügel*

animal	cat	fowl	octopus	snake
bear	cattle	goat	owl	swan
bird	deer	horse	pig	wolf
butterfly	eagle	insect	sheep	

Neuter Gender

bag	chimney	kettle	seat
book	desk	mirror	stairs
box	dishes	pillow	street
bread	floor	ruler	table
chalk	house	school	wall

2. Main Verbs

A. *Kinds of Verbs*

There are two types of verbs in English: Main Verbs and Auxiliary Verbs. Main verbs are either **regular** (play, like, press) or **irregular** (drink, buy), though irregular verbs are not completely irregular.

(a) *Regular Verbs.* The great majority of English verbs are regular; that is, they have four forms:

The base (the uninflected or unchanged form)	play
The -*s* form	plays
The -*ing* form	playing
The -*ed* form	played

The **base form** is used:

1. in the present tense with all persons except the third person singular

$$\left.\begin{array}{l} \text{I} \\ \text{You} \\ \text{We} \\ \text{They} \end{array}\right\} \; \textit{like coffee.}$$

2. in the imperative: *Telephone* immediately.
3. in the infinitive:

I saw him *play* football yesterday. (bare infinitive)
I want you *to clean* the bedroom. (*to-* infinitive)

The -*s* **form** is called the **third person singular present**. In both regular and irregular verbs it is formed by adding -*s* or -*es* to the base. In spoken English the -*s* form is pronounced /s/, /iz/, or /z/:

Base	*-s form*	
call	calls	/z/
wash	washes	/iz/
help	helps	/s/

$$\left.\begin{array}{l} \text{He} \\ \text{She} \\ \text{It} \end{array}\right\} \; \text{likes water.}$$

Changes of spelling occur with some words (see page 114).

The *-ing* **form** is called the **present participle.** In both regular and irregular verbs it is formed by adding *-ing* to the base:

Base	*-ing form*
call	calling
wash	washing
help	helping

Changes of spelling also occur with some verbs (see pages 114-15).

The *-ed* **form** of regular verbs is formed by adding *-ed* to the base. In spoken English the *-ed* form is pronounced /id/, /d/, or /t/:

Base	*-ed form*	
call	called	/d/
wash	washed	/t/
paint	painted	/id/

Changes of spelling occur with some verbs, e.g. pat/patted. (See pages 114-15.) The *-ed* form is used:

1. in the past tense in all persons:

I
You
He/She ⎬ washed the car.
They

2. with a form of the verb 'to be' to form the passive (see page 39):

He *was killed* in the train crash.

3. with a form of the verb 'to have' to form the past perfect tense:

She *has painted* the room white.

(b) *Irregular Verbs.* The irregular main verbs in the English language are small in number but important in function. They resemble regular verbs in having regular *-s* and *-ing* forms, but they differ from regular verbs in that sometimes the **base form** changes in the past form and/or past participle form.

There are three types of irregular verbs:
1. Verbs in which all three parts (the base, the past, the past participle) are identical: let—let—let.
2. Verbs in which two of the three parts are identical: build—built—built.
3. Verbs in which all three parts are different: speak—spoke—spoken.

23

Below is a list of irregular verbs corresponding to the three groupings above. They are grouped according to similarity. If there is an acceptable regular form, that has been included along with its irregular counterpart.

Verbs in which all three parts are identical

Base Form	The Past Form	The Past Participle Form
bet	bet/betted	bet/betted
bid	bid	bid
broadcast	broadcast	broadcast
burst	burst	burst
cast	cast	cast
cost	cost	cost
cut	cut	cut
hit	hit	hit
hurt	hurt	hurt
knit	knit/knitted	knit/knitted
let	let	let
put	put	put
quit	quit/quitted	quit/quitted
read /riːd/	read /red/	read /red/
set	set	set
shut	shut	shut
split	split	split
spread	spread	spread
thrust	thrust	thrust
wed	wed/wedded	wed/wedded

Verbs in which two parts are identical

beat	beat	beaten
become	became	become
bend	bent	bent
bind	bound	bound
bleed	bled	bled
breed	bred	bred
bring	brought	brought
build	built	built
burn	burned/burnt	burned/burnt
buy	bought	bought
catch	caught	caught
cling	clung	clung
come	came	come
creep	crept	crept
dig	dug	dug
dream	dreamt/dreamed	dreamt/dreamed
feed	fed	fed
feel	felt	felt

24

fight	fought	fought
find	found	found
flee	fled	fled
fling	flung	flung
get	got	got
grind	ground	ground
hang	hung	hung
	hanged (= suspended by the neck)	
have	had	had
hear	heard	heard
hold	held	held
keep	kept	kept
kneel	kneeled/knelt	kneeled/knelt
lay	laid	laid
lead	led	led
leap	leaped/leapt	leaped/leapt
learn	learned/learnt	learned/learnt
leave	left	left
lend	lent	lent
light	lighted/lit	lighted/lit
lose	lost	lost
make	made	made
mean	meant	meant
meet	met	met
mislay	mislaid	mislaid
overcome	overcame	overcame
pay	paid	paid
run	ran	run
say	said	said
seek	sought	sought
sell	sold	sold
send	sent	sent
shoot	shot	shot
sit	sat	sat
sleep	slept	slept
slide	slid	slid
smell	smelled/smelt	smelled/smelt
speed	sped	sped
spell	spelled/spelt	spelled/spelt
spend	spent	spent
spill	spilled/spilt	spilled/spilt
stand	stood	stood
stick	stuck	stuck
strike	struck	struck
string	strung	strung
sweep	swept	swept
swing	swung	swung
teach	taught	taught
tell	told	told
think	thought	thought

understand	understood	understood
weep	wept	wept
win	won	won
wind	wound	wound
withhold	withheld	withheld
withstand	withstood	withstood
wring	wrung	wrung

Verbs in which all three parts are different

arise	arose	arisen
(a)wake	(a)woke	(a)woken/(a)waked
be	was	been
bear	bore	born/borne
begin	began	begun
bite	bit	bitten
blow	blew	blown
break	broke	broken
choose	chose	chosen
do	did	done
draw	drew	drawn
drink	drank	drunk
drive	drove	driven
eat	ate	eaten
fall	fell	fallen
fly	flew	flown
forbid	forbade	forbidden
forget	forgot	forgotten
freeze	froze	frozen
give	gave	given
go	went	gone
grow	grew	grown
hide	hid	hid/hidden
know	knew	known
lie	lay	lain
mistake	mistook	mistaken
ride	rode	ridden
ring	rang	rung
rise	rose	risen
saw	sawed	sawed/sawn
see	saw	seen
shake	shook	shaken
show	showed	showed/shown
sing	sang	sung
sink	sank	sunk
speak	spoke	spoken
spring	sprang	sprung
steal	stole	stolen
swear	swore	sworn
swim	swam	swum

26

take	took	taken
tear	tore	torn
throw	threw	thrown
undergo	underwent	undergone
wear	wore	worn
weave	wove	woven
withdraw	withdrew	withdrawn
write	wrote	written

B. *Verb Patterns*

There are six basic verb patterns in English and a larger number of sub-patterns. These are listed below, together with examples:

(a) *Linking Verbs.* In this pattern, the verb is a linking verb. Such verbs usually describe a state or condition:

appear (satisfied)	stay (young)	grow (old)
feel (ill)	smell (sweet)	fall (sick)
look (pretty)	sound (angry)	run (wild)
seem (happy)	taste (sour)	turn (bitter)

Linking verbs form the following patterns:

1. Verb + Noun or Verb + (to be) Noun: The complement is a noun phrase or nominal clause.	She *is* a very attractive woman. He *became* a Professor of Physics. He *seems* (to be) a very bright child.
2. Verb + Adjective or Verb + (to be) Adjective: The complement is an adjective.	Your hair *looks* nice. He *sounded* furious over the phone.
3. Verb + Necessary Adverbial: The verb is followed by an adverbial.	Mother *is* at home. She *leaned* out of the window. The meeting *lasted* two hours. The flowers *cost* one dollar.

(b) *Verbs with One Object (Transitive Verbs)*

1. Verb + Noun: The object is a noun phrase.	He *poisoned* the cat. Everybody *sang* the national anthem. She *tidied* the house.
2. Verb + Bare Infinitive: The verb is used with a bare infinitive (i.e. without *to*).	May I *help* with the dishes?

27

3. Verb + *to-* infinitive: The object is a *to-* infinitive.

She *agreed* to write to her aunt.
They *decided* to go for a swim.

4. Verb + *-ing* form: The verb is followed by an *-ing* form. Such verbs include:

He *denied* causing the accident.
She *disliked* going to music lessons.

avoid	consider	finish
miss	deny	postpone
dislike	risk	enjoy

5. Verb + *that-* clause: The verb has a *that-* clause (where *that* can be omitted). Verbs:

I *admit* (that) he is a good lecturer.
You *forget* (that) I am your father.

accept	claim	understand
admit	doubt	discover
feel	forget	recommend
demand	insist	require

6. Verb + *wh-* word: The verb has a clause introduced by a *wh-* word: how, why, where, who, whether, if. Verbs:

I *wonder* $\left\{ \begin{array}{c} \text{if} \\ \text{whether} \end{array} \right\}$ she will come.
He still doesn't *know* how to tie his shoelaces.

decide	forget	discuss
guess	doubt	wonder

(c) *Verbs with Object + Verb (+ . . .)*: These transitive verbs have an object which is followed by another verb.

1. Verb + Object + Bare Infinitive: The verb and object are followed by an infinitive without *to*.

Shall I *help* you carry that box?
We *felt* the house shake.
You *made* me spill my tea.

2. Verb + Object + *to-* infinitive: Verbs:

She *asked* the maid to wash the floor.
They *advised* us to stay in our seats.

ask	advise	cause
get	allow	forget
require	teach	tell
urge	order	intend

3. Verb + Object + *-ing* form:

They *saw* the thief running away.
Can you *smell* something burning?
She could *feel* her heart beating.

28

| 4. Verb + Object + -*ed* form: | We *found* the house deserted.
I *want* the work finished by noon. *(to be)*
He couldn't *make* himself heard. |

(d) *Verbs with Two Objects*

1. Verb + Noun + Noun: Verb + indirect object + direct object. Verbs:

| | | | She *gave* the door a hard kick.
She *owed* him a thousand dollars.
May I *ask* you a favour? |

'to' verbs:

bring	give	hand
offer	owe	promise
read	send	show
take	teach	write

'for' verbs:

| cook | find | get |
| learn | make | save |

> She *gave* her mother the gloves.
> She *gave* the gloves *to* her mother.
> She *cooked* her father a meal.
> She *cooked* a meal *for* her father.

Note: The above pattern may be replaced by a *direct object + to/for + noun phrase.*

2. Verb + Object + a *that*- clause (where *that* is often omitted): Verbs:

| assure | convince | persuade |
| remind | inform | tell |

I *convinced* him that I was innocent.
We must *remind* him that he's on duty tonight.
The workers *told* the employers that they wanted more money.

3. Verb + Object + a *wh*- clause (or *how*- clause):

She *told* me why she had come.
Tell me what your name is.
This *shows* how wrong you were.

4. Verb + Object + *wh*- word + *to*- infinitive:

I can't *decide* what to do next.
I'll *enquire* how to get there.
I *showed* her where to sit.

(e) *Verbs with Object and Object Complement*

1. Verb + Noun + Noun Phrase (where the complement is a noun phrase):

OR

Verb + Noun + (to be) Noun: 'to be' may appear before the noun phrase complement.

He *ordered* himself a bottle of wine.
She *made* her mother a new dress.
Can you *spare* me a few minutes of your time?
He *found* her (to be) a very hardworking colleague.
They *appointed* him (to be) the tennis coach.

29

Verbs:

appoint	imagine	found
consider	suppose	think

2. Verb + Noun + Adjective (where the complement is an adjective):
Verbs:

paint	serve	leave
make	keep	wash

He *left* the apartment filthy.
He *painted* his car black.

OR

Verb + Noun + (to be) Adjective: 'to be' may appear before the adjective complement.
Verbs:

feel	think	know
imagine	believe	suppose

They *imagined* him (to be) crazy.
Many students *thought* the exam (to be) unfair.

3. Verb + Object + Necessary <u>Adverbial</u>: The verb has an adverbial following the object.

Please *put* the milk in the refrigerator.
They *kept* their daughter indoors.
The detective *followed* the <u>suspect</u> for two hours.

(f) *Verbs without Object or Complement (Intransitive Verbs)*

1. Verb + *to*- infinitive: Verbs with no object or complement.
Note: (i) It may be a phrasal verb without an object.
(ii) The missing object is understood.

She *cried*.
The dress *fits*.

The heater *blew up*.
The fugitive *gave up*.

Chris *smokes*. (understood object = cigarettes)

2. Verb + *-ing* Form:

They *went* jogging.
She *came* visiting.

C. *Tense and Aspect*

   Tense refers to the form a verb takes depending on the time at which an action occurred. Tenses may indicate whether an action, activity, or state took place in the present, past or future. Tenses may also indicate whether an action, activity, or state is, was, or will be complete, or

30

whether it is, was, or will be in progress over a period of time. This is called **Aspect**.

There are two simple tenses in English: The **Present Tense** and the **Past Tense**. There are also two main aspects in English: The **Progressive** (or Continuous) **Aspect** and the **Perfect Aspect**.

The two tenses above can combine with the two aspects to form several combinations:

Present Time	The Simple Present	She always *bakes* nice cakes.
	The Present Progressive (Continuous)	She *is baking* a cake now.
Past Time	The Simple Past	She *baked* a cake for her family yesterday.
	The Past Progressive (Continuous)	She *was baking* a cake when her husband came home.
	The Present Perfect	She *has baked* several cakes for her friends.
	The Present Perfect Progressive (Continuous)	She *has been baking* cakes all morning.
	The Past Perfect	She *had baked* three cakes by midday.
	The Past Perfect Progressive (Continuous)	She *had been baking* cakes all morning and felt hot and tired.

Future time is also expressed in a variety of ways.

The above are the **active** tenses and aspects. For notes on the **passive** see page 39.

Tense, however, is not as straightforward as the table above suggests, because a verb may have different kinds of meaning depending, for instance, on whether it is referring to a single, completed action or a series of repeated actions or a temporary state of affairs, etc.

Below is a description of when each of the tenses is used:

(a) *The Simple Present Tense*
1. expresses repeated action (includes the past, present and future)

It *rains* every day.
The earth *revolves* around the sun.
She *travels* to work by bus.

31

2. expresses non-action (of a state or condition) or indefinite occurrences

She *seems* ill.
He *loves* his pets.
I *remember* him.

3. expresses special short-term events

I *declare* this seminar open.
I *resign*.

4. expresses future action (especially with verbs of arriving and departing) based on facts or certain events

They *leave* tomorrow.
The ship *sails* on Thursday.
The play *begins* at 7 p.m. on Sunday.

(b) *The Present Progressive (Continuous) Tense*

1. expresses one action in the present
   (i) of short duration

I *am writing* a report.
The boys *are playing* tennis at the club.

   (ii) of long duration

She's *writing* a children's book.
He's *studying* Mandarin this term.
Joe's *playing* cricket this season.

2. expresses future action (often resulting from a present plan or arrangement)

He *is going* to France next year.
She *is washing* her hair tonight.
The ship *is sailing* next week.

3. expresses the beginning, progression or end of an action

It *is beginning* to rain.
My cold *is getting* worse.

(c) *The Simple Past Tense*

1. expresses a definite, completed action or event

I *wrote* him a <u>note of thanks</u> for the gift.
We *had* dinner at seven o'clock last night.
I *saw* him in September, 1976.

2. expresses a series of actions happening over a certain period of time

She *practised* the violin every day for five years.
She *studied* linguistics while she was in California.
All last year he *prepared* for the music examination.

32

3. expresses a state of affairs continuing over a period of time with no clear beginning and end	I *lived* in India during my childhood. In Columbus's day, people *believed* that the earth was flat.

(d) *The Past Progressive (Continuous) Tense*

1. expresses duration of an action or single event in the past	
(i) of short duration	They *were eating* in the cafeteria a few minutes ago. We *were watching* TV all evening. He *was thinking* about the accident all night long.
(ii) interrupted by a non-continuous past action	He *was working* in a restaurant last time I *met* him. She *was washing* the dishes when the phone *rang*. They *were watching* television when the lights *went out*.
2. expresses an incomplete action in the past that is itself likely to be of limited duration	The family *was eating* dinner. The children *were playing* in the street. They *were arguing* about who would win the election.

(e) *The Present Perfect Tense*

1. expresses actions or a series of repeated events that extend from the past to the present time (but which are still continuing)	I *have studied* English for six years. They *have lived* in Thailand since 1970. I *have visited* the museum three times so far.
2. expresses indefinite events or happenings in a period leading up to the present time	The children *have had* colds all winter. We *have had* no trouble with our car up to now.
3. expresses past actions or events with results in the present time	The landlord *has called* for the <u>rent</u> (and so you must pay it). I *have come* to school without my glasses (and now I cannot see).

33

(f) *The Present Perfect Progressive (Continuous) Tense*

1. expresses a single temporary action that extends from the past to the present—over a limited period of time

> She *has been waiting* to see you since one o'clock.
> I *have been waiting* all day for his telephone call.
> He *has been watering* the garden for an hour.

2. expresses a series of repeated actions from the past up to the present time—over a longer period of time

> I *have been playing* the piano since I was five.
> He *has been working* for the same company for the last twenty-five years.
> He *has been seeing* a great deal of his girlfriend lately.

3. expresses an action that happens in the past but the results of the action happen in the present

> The boys *have been playing* football (and now they're filthy).
> Watch out! Mike *has been painting* the door (and it's still wet).

(g) *The Past Perfect Tense*

1. expresses a single happening in past time that precedes another past time

> They *had locked* all the doors before they left.
> The thieves *had* already *gone* before the police arrived.
> After she *had spoken*, she realized her mistake.

2. expresses a state of affairs continuing over a period of time up to past time

> I *had known* her since childhood.
> He *had* never *been ill* in his life until he visited Asia.

(h) *The Past Perfect Progressive (Continuous) Tense*

expresses duration of a single event or happening up to the past time

> They *had been trying* to reach us by phone all day.
> They *had been planning* for a long time to move to the city.
> She *had been studying* for several hours before she realized she was hungry.

(i) *Future Time*

There are several ways to express future time:

1. the auxiliaries *will* and *shall* express future of prediction

> He *will call* you tomorrow.
> The plane *will arrive* at 10 p.m.
> I *shall meet* you outside the library.

34

2. *be going to* + infinitive expresses the idea of intention or expectation to future time

My children *are going to plan* their holiday this year.
He *is going to call* you tomorrow.
They *are going to fly* to London in a few days.

3. the present progressive (continuous) tense (see page 32) expresses future actions often resulting from a present plan or arrangement

I'm going to the office by bus next week.
She *is baking* a cake tonight.
The team *is leaving* tomorrow.

4. the simple present tense (see page 31), together with a future time expression, expresses future action based on facts or certain events

They *return* from France next week.
The shop *closes* soon.
He *starts* university in September.

5. the auxiliaries *will* and *shall* + the progressive (continuous) tense are used for a single action especially if it has duration

He *will be getting* a raise in salary soon.
We *will be having* a party tomorrow night.
I *will be finishing* my examination at five o'clock.

6. the future perfect tense (*will/shall* + the perfect) expresses a future time that precedes another future time

In January we *will have been married* ten years.
In ten years we *will have paid off* the mortgage on our house.
By next year he *will have forgotten* everything he learned in class.

I've been **stuck** on this crossword for two hours!

At this rate I'll **never finish** it!

What **I need** is a talking dictionary!

D. *Avoiding Errors with Tenses*

1. When in doubt as to whether or not to use the Simple Past Tense or the Past Perfect, remember that the past tense refers to a **definite time** in the past whereas the Past Perfect is used to express a past action that took place before another past action.

2. The past tense is usually indicated by:
   (a) a past time adverbial in the same sentence:

   > My parents lived in Singapore *during the Japanese Occupation.*
   > I was born *in 1946.*
   > He studied Tagalog *while he was in the Philippines.*

   (b) The context of the language before the sentence.
   (c) The context outside language:

   > *Did* the postman *bring* any letters?

3. Whereas the Past Tense uses adverbials expressing definite time (yesterday, in June, at 4 o'clock, last year), the Past Perfect uses adverbials that express past-to-present time:

since, for	I have lived here *for* four years. I have lived here *since* 1979.
so far, up to now, up to the present	We have had no trouble with our TV set *so far*.
frequency words: always, never, ever, often, sometimes, occasionally	He has *always* lived in this town. This is the best book I have *ever* read on birds. He has *occasionally* come late to class.
just, already, finally	Our dinner guests have *just* arrived.
recently, lately	She has not seen him *recently*.

   Note: Some adverbials go with both tenses:

$$I \left\{ \begin{array}{l} \text{saw} \\ \text{have seen} \end{array} \right\} \text{her} \left\{ \begin{array}{l} \text{today.} \\ \text{this week/month/year.} \\ \text{recently.} \end{array} \right.$$

$$\left. \begin{array}{l} \text{I always/never forget} \\ \text{I have always/never forgotten} \end{array} \right\} \text{my parents' wedding anniversary}$$

4. Because the progressive (or continuous) usually emphasizes duration of a single event, the adverbials just, already, ever, never, finally, are not generally used (as these suggest definiteness and finality).

5. Verbs which are commonly used with the progressive aspect include verbs denoting:
activities: drink, read, walk, work, write, etc.
processes: change, grow, improve, widen, etc.
momentary events that suggest repetition: jump, kick, knock, nod, etc.

6. Some verbs cannot take the progressive aspect because they do not suggest an action in progress:
Verbs of perceiving: feel, hear, see, smell, taste. *Note*: exceptions: when these state verbs become activity verbs or mental activity verbs;

> The doctor *is feeling* her pulse.
> I*'ve been tasting* the curry.
> I*'ve been thinking* about the film I saw last night.

Verbs referring to a state of mind or feeling: adore, believe, hope, dislike, know, love, understand, wish, etc.
Verbs referring to a relationship or a state of being: belong to, concern, consist of, depend on, involve, possess, remain, require.

7. A main verb in the present or future may be followed by a verb in any tense, but a main verb in the past must be followed by a verb in the past:

present	The prisoner *says*	that he *is* innocent. that he *told* the truth in court. that he *will be* out of jail soon.
future	The prisoner *will say*	that he *is* innocent. that he *told* the truth in court. that he *will be* out of jail soon.
past	The prisoner *said*	that he *was* innocent. that he *had told* the truth in court. that he *would be* out of jail soon.

8. *Rules for Subject and Verb Agreement (Concord)*
'Concord' here means that verbs must agree in number with the nouns in a sentence.

Rule 1: In English, number concord only affects present tense verbs plus the past tense of 'be'.	I *walk*, he *walks* He *was*, they *were*

Rule 2: Usually singular subjects take singular verbs; plural subjects take plural verbs.

He *runs* fast; They *run* fast, etc.
The girl *was* singing.
Where *is* the boy hiding?

Rule 3: Two or more singular subjects joined by *and* take a plural verb.

Fog, smoke, *and* heavy snow *cancel* scheduled flights.

Rule 4:

(i) Singular subjects separated by *or, nor*, and *either . . . or* take a singular verb.

Either the television *or* the newspaper *is* a good source for news.
Neither the driver *nor* the co-driver *feels* sleepy.

(ii) Plural subjects separated by *or, nor* take a plural verb.

Neither the teachers *nor* the parents *are* to blame.

(iii) When two noun phrases are joined by *or* or *either . . . or*, and one has a plural subject, generally the number of the verb is determined by the number of the *last* noun phrase.

Neither the inspector nor his officers *were* able to help us.

Rule 5: Phrases separating the subject and verb do not influence the number of the subject. A subject following the verb still agrees in number with the verb.

Here *comes* mother now.
Here *come* mother and father now.
There *goes* that funny man next door.
Do the watchman and his son cycle to work together?

Rule 6: Context determines the number of collective nouns (see page 11), e.g. team, audience, family, group.

(i) When the members of a collective noun act as individuals, the verb is plural.

The team *are* discussing next year's schedule.
The audience *were* taking turns to give donations to the fund.

(ii) When the members of a collective noun act as a unit, the verb is singular.

The team *wins* every game *it* plays on its home ground.
The audience *was* cheering the band.

Rule 7: Plural words and phrases count as singular if they are used as names, titles, quotations, etc.

The Munsters was my favourite television show.
Biggles of the Interpol is one of W. E. Johns's more exciting children's books.

Rule 8: Words plural in form but singular in meaning take a singular verb (see page 14).

Linguistics *is* the study of language.
The news from the war front *is* alarming.

E. *The Passive*

Many verbs can be used to make statements about the same event in two different ways:

Active voice: The man (subject) opened the door (object).
Passive voice: The door (original object) was opened by the man (original subject).

The term **passive** then consists of a form of **be + past participle**, e.g. was harmed, was spoilt, was seen. The opposite of passive is **active**.

Because an original object becomes the grammatical subject in a passive statement, only transitive verbs (i.e. verbs that take an object) may be used in the passive voice.

1. The passive voice can be formed with all tenses and aspects:

Tense	Active Voice	Passive Voice
Simple present	offer, offers	am / is / are } offered
Present progressive	am / is / are } offering	am / is / are } being offered
Simple past	offered	was / were } offered
Past progressive	was / were } offering	was / were } being offered
Future	shall / will } offer	shall / will } be offered
Present perfect	has / have } offered	has / have } been offered
Past perfect	had offered	had been offered
Future perfect	shall / will } have offered	shall / will } have been offered

2. Conversion from the active to the passive:
   (a) Except for a few instances, all active sentences with a noun phrase or pronoun object, can be converted to the passive.
   (b) There are three steps in the conversion of an active clause into a passive clause:
   (i) by replacing the active verb phrase by the matching passive one;
   (ii) by making the object of the active clause the subject of the passive clause;
   (iii) by making the subject of the active clause, the agent (or 'doer' of the action) of the passive clause.

   The three steps can be illustrated as follows:

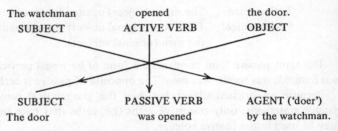

The watchman	opened	the door.
SUBJECT	ACTIVE VERB	OBJECT

SUBJECT	PASSIVE VERB	AGENT ('doer')
The door	was opened	by the watchman.

   (c) The sentences below illustrate the above process. Note the different kinds of verb patterns that are changed:

	ACTIVE		PASSIVE
SVO	The boy *opened* the door.	→ SV (passive) *by-* agent	The door *was opened* by the boy.
SVOV	His landlord *asked* him to leave.	→ SV (passive) V *by-* agent	He *was asked* to leave by his landlord.
SVOO	The waiter *handed* him the bill.	→ SV (passive) O *by-* agent	He *was handed* the the bill by the waiter. OR The bill was given to him by the waiter.
SVOC	They *considered* the house too expensive.	→ SV (passive) C *by-*agent	The house *was considered* too expensive (by them).

What has happened in the above sentences is that the noun phrases acting as subject and object in the active sentences become reversed in the passive sentences.

Note:

1. The *by-* phrase + agent is only required in certain cases and is not used in many English passive sentences.
2. The passive voice is preferred in English when the 'doer' of an action is unimportant or unknown. Because of its impersonal tone it is commonly found in textbooks, in scientific, technical and business reports, and in newspaper accounts:

   The lectures *will be given* by Mr Jim Freeman.
   Two policemen *were killed* last night in a clash with terrorists.

3. The agent ('doer') is often omitted in passive sentences, especially when it is obvious enough who the agent is. This omission again adds to the impersonal style of the passive:

   The house *is painted* every year.
   The proposal *is being considered*.
   All the examination results *will be posted* on the notice board next week.
   The matter *has already been investigated*.

3. Adjectives

An adjective is a word that **modifies**, or changes, the meaning of a noun or pronoun. It may point out, describe or limit the meaning of the noun or pronoun.

A. *Characteristics of Adjectives*

1. The majority of adjectives can be both (i) attributive or descriptive (He's an *intelligent* child), and (ii) predicative (All her children are *intelligent*).
2. Most of them can also be modified by intensifiers, e.g. fairly, rather, quite, very.
3. Most can also take comparative and superlative forms when used for degrees of comparison.

B. *Kinds of Adjectives and their Functions*

(a) *Attributive (or Descriptive) Adjectives*

1. As the name suggests, attributive adjectives attribute some quality to a person or thing. As such, they are placed after the determiners (see page 67) but before the noun which is head of a phrase.
2. Attributive adjectives include those that are generally descriptive, i.e. assign qualities (*beautiful*, *intelligent*, *clear*) or physical states

of size, shape, age, colour, temperature, as well as proper adjectives referring to nationalities, geographical places, religions, holidays, dates, names, titles, etc., e.g. *Italian* food, *Parisian* styles, *Christian* beliefs.

3. Although most adjectives can be either attributive or predicative, some can only be used in the attributive position; i.e. before a noun adjunct or a noun, e.g. a *former* tenant, the *late* prime minister, an *occasional* drink, a *hard* worker, a *big* liar, a *Buddhist* monk.

4. Some attributive adjectives are derived from nouns, e.g. a *law* school, a *flower* garden, the *weather* forecast, *criminal* law, an *atomic* scientist, *pay*-day, *air*mail.

5. Sequence of Adjectives before Nouns:

Determiners 1	Attributive (Descriptive) Adjectives 2			Noun Adjuncts 3	Nouns 4
	general description (qualities)	physical state (size, shape, age, temperature, colour)	proper adjectives (nationalities, religions, etc.)		
both the	air-conditioned	black	Mercedes Benz		cars
a	beautiful		farming		district
those four	multi-purpose	aluminium		kitchen	utensils
a	steep	muddy		river	bank
all those	angry	young			men
a		very large	Buddhist		temple
her	low-cut		Parisian	evening	dress

(b) *Predicative Adjectives*

1. Such adjectives act as complements of verbs:
   (i) as subject complements after linking verbs like *be*, *seem*, *look*, *feel*

   You look *happy* this morning.
   Patent leather is *smooth* and *shiny*.

42

(ii) as object complements after verbs like *believe, find, consider*

They considered him the *best* architect.
We found the park *delightful*.

(iii) as a complement to a subject which is a finite clause or non-finite clause

Whether the mail will come is *unclear*.
Riding a skateboard isn't as *easy* as you may imagine.

(iv) as object complements to clauses

Most girls consider their boyfriends *good-looking*.

2. Some groups of adjectives can only be used in the predicative position, e.g. health adjectives—She felt *ill*; He felt *faint*.

(c) *Post-modifying Adjectives*

Adjectives, in particular predicative adjectives, are sometimes post-modifiers (i.e. they follow the word they modify):
1. as a reduced relative clause

Was there anything (which was) *interesting* on the news?
The people (who were) *involved* were punished.

2. as post-modifiers in compounds

court *martial*, postmaster *general*

(d) *Participle Adjectives*

A large number of adjectives have the same form as *-ing* or *-ed* participles:

His ideas on religion are *astonishing*.
She seemed *satisfied* with my explanation.

Such adjectives can also be attributive: his *astonishing* ideas.

(e) *Adjectives as Heads*

Some adjectives can function as heads of noun phrases:
1. adjectives denoting a class or group of people (plural)

The *rich* can afford to eat meat every day.
The *unemployed* suffer most in times of inflation.

Note that a definite article precedes such adjectives.
2. adjectives denoting an abstract quality

Many people study the *supernatural* in folklore.

43

C. *Adjective Patterns*

There are three main types of adjective patterns:

(a) *Adjective + prepositional phrase*

The meaning of an adjective is often completed by the use of a prepositional phrase: afraid of, angry with, pleased about, etc. Usually the preposition is fixed by an idiom (see page 141) but there may be a choice of preposition (see page 141).

> You must be more *accurate in* your work.
> Doctors say that milk is *good for* you.
> You are *interested in* yoga, aren't you?

(b) *Adjectives + that- clause*

A *that-* clause is used as a complement following:
1. personal subjects

> Are you sure that he's *honest*?
> She's *surprised* that you're going abroad.

Note: Other adjectives and participles that take *that-* clauses: sure, glad, certain, confident, proud, sad, alarmed, annoyed, pleased, shocked.

2. introductory 'It' as the subject

> It's *sad* that he is so ill.
> It's *fortunate* that he only took her radio.

(e) *Adjective + to- infinitive*

The adjectives used in this pattern are followed by a *to-* infinitive. Some can be recomposed:

> The house was *difficult* to find. It was *difficult* to find the house.
> It's *easy* to please Father. Father is *easy* to please.
> She was *careful* not to step in the puddle.
> It's *good* to eat fresh peaches again.

D. *Comparison of Adjectives*

Gradable adjectives have three degrees of comparison:

> The **Positive Degree**, used when no comparison is made;
> The **Comparative Degree**, used when two things are compared;
> The **Superlative Degree**, used when more than two things are compared.

44

Comparison is expressed by the endings -er and -est or by the words **more** and **most**.

The endings are generally used with the following:

-er than	: comparative	more than	: comparative
the -est	: superlative	the most	: superlative

1. adjectives with one syllable:
   tall—taller than—the tallest

2. adjectives with two syllables
   ending in:
   -y   dirtier than, the dirtiest
   -le   gentler than, the gentlest
   -er   cleverer than, the
         cleverest
   -ow   shallower than, the
         shallowest

1. adjectives with three or more
   syllables:
   beautiful—more beautiful than—
   the most beautiful

2. two-syllable adjectives with
   derivational endings (-ful, -less,
   -ish, -ous, -ing, -ed, etc.)
   more useful than, the most useful
   more famous than, the most
   famous
   more frightening than, the most
   frightening

Two-syllable adjectives with either form:
— some adjectives ending in -er (clever)
— adjectives ending in -ow (narrow)
— adjectives ending in -some (handsome)
— others: polite, sincere, severe, common,
  pleasant, cruel, quiet, stupid

Note: In adding -er or -est for comparison, keep in mind that:
(a) Final y preceded by a consonant is changed to i, e.g. livelier, tastier
(b) A final single consonant preceded by a single vowel is doubled, e.g.
    bigger, thinner, hottest.
(c) Final e is dropped, e.g. simpler, larger, widest.

Irregular comparison. Note the forms of the following irregular adjectives:

Positive	Comparative	Superlative
good	better	best
bad	worse	worst
far	farther (for distance)	farthest
	further (for information)	furthest
little	less	least
much	more	most

45

4. Adverbs

A. *Formation of Adverbs*

1. Most adverbs in English are derived from adjectives by the addition of *-ly*:

Adjective	Adverb
quick	quick*ly*
loud	loud*ly*
slow	slow*ly*
neat	neat*ly*

2. Some adverbs, however, do not end in *-ly*, but have exactly the same form as adjectives. Such adverbs are mostly concerned with time, position, and direction:

Adjective	Adverb
an *early* dinner	We ate dinner *early* last night.
a *late* lunch	I worked *late* at the office.
a *hard* task	I tried *hard* to stop him.
a *long* journey	I can't stay very *long*.
a *high* fence	Don't jump too *high*.
a *short* rest	The donations fell *short* of the target.
a *direct* telephone line	My brother flew *direct* to London.
a *straight* line	I went *straight* to the director.

3. In some cases, there is also an adverb ending in *-ly*, but with a different meaning from its adjectival form:

Adjective	Adverb
late (= after the expected time)	He hasn't been here *lately*. (= recently)
direct (= straight)	The doctor will see you *directly*. (= soon)
	He drove home *directly* after receiving the news. (= immediately)
short (= opposite of long or tall)	I will be meeting him *shortly*. (= soon/in a short while)
hard (= firm and stiff; difficult, etc.)	He can *hardly* be considered for the position. (= barely; to be unlikely)

46

| strong (= powerful) | He felt *strongly* about the drug situation in the country. (= very concerned) |

4. Sometimes adjectives and adverbs have almost the same meaning although the form of the word differs. In such instances, the adverbs represent more formal usage.

> He buys his shoes *cheap/cheaply* at a second-hand shop.
> She spoke *clear/clearly*.
> We had to drive *slow/slowly* in the rain.
> The baby lay *quiet/quietly* in his cot.

B. Types of Adverbs
There are several kinds of adverbs:

(a) *Adverbs of Time*. These answer the question 'When?': now, soon, already, today, before, ago, then, immediately, lately, yesterday.
   There are three kinds of Time Adverbs:
   1. expressing **a definite time period**:
      yesterday, now, last year, today
   2. expressing **duration/length of time**:
      lately, since, always, temporarily
   3. expressing **frequency**:
      (i) **definite**: every day, weekly, monthly, twice, etc.
      (ii) **indefinite**: sometimes, regularly, always, normally, occasionally, seldom, usually, never, frequently

(b) *Adverbs of Place and Direction*. These answer the question 'Where?': here, there, everywhere, in, out, above, down, behind, below, outside, left, straight, west, etc.

(c) *Adverbs of Manner, Means and Instrument*. These answer the question 'How?', 'In what way/manner?': surely, better, easily, well, quietly, loudly, politely, badly, awkwardly, etc.

(d) *Adverbs of Degree*. These answer the question 'How much?', 'To what extent?', 'To what degree?': very, quite, so, too, rather, almost, completely, entirely, less, thoroughly, even, only, scarcely, hardly, etc.
Note: These adverbs can show both intensity of degree (very, quite) as well as emphasis (even, only).

(e) *Conjunctive Adverbs*. These adverbs modify a sentence: therefore, nevertheless.

47

(f) *Sentence Adverbs*. These are not an important part of the sentence structure; they often have a connective role. They often convey the speaker's comment on the content of what he is saying, e.g. fortunately, actually, admittedly, certainly, indeed, naturally, surely, perhaps, in fact, really, hopefully, luckily, surprisingly, etc.

C. *Functions of Adverbs*

Adverbs have two major functions and one minor function:

Major functions:
(a) as *adverbials* (or adverb word groups)
(b) as *modifiers* of adjectives, adverbs and other constructions

Minor function:
(c) as *complements* of prepositions

(a) *Adverbs as Adverbials*. The function of adverbials is to tell us something additional about an action, happening, or state described in the sentence:

Adverbs of Time 1. definite time period	The match starts *today at 4 p.m.* They are *now* holidaying in Manila.
2. duration/length of time	He's been working on the report *since last July*. My father is *temporarily* out of a job.
3. frequency: — definite	I'll be at the office *every day* this week. He goes away on business *twice a month*.
— indefinite	I *seldom* get up before 8 a.m. Do they *normally* have their meals at restaurants?
Adverbs of Place and Direction	I can't find my glasses *anywhere*. In Malaysia, children play badminton *outside*.
Adverbs of Manner, Means, and Instrument	The building was *formally* opened by the Prime Minister. He phrased the question *awkwardly*.

48

Adverbs of Degree	She cleaned the spare room *thoroughly*. He *nearly* missed the train.
Conjunctive Adverbs	There's a tear in this dress: *thus*, I want my money back.
Sentence Adverbs	A bus and a taxi collided at the junction; *happily*, no one was injured.

(b) *Adverbs as Modifiers*. The function of these adverbs is to modify or affect the meaning of other word classes. Such adverbs are usually *degree adverbs*: they express intensity and emphasis in a sentence.

They act as modifiers of the following word classes:

1. as modifiers of adjectives: very, quite, rather, extremely	It is *extremely* good of you to do my marketing. He's *rather* clever for a five-year old. It was an *absolutely* awful film.
2. as modifiers of other adverbs: very, rather, quite	He is sleeping *very* soundly. He was drinking *rather* heavily after his son died.
3. as modifiers of determiners, pronouns or numerals: hardly, nearly, over, enough	She has *hardly* any relatives. *Nearly* everyone failed the entrance test. *Over* twenty thousand teenagers poured into the stadium.
4. as modifiers of prepositional phrases: right, dead	The rain went *right* through the roof. I am *dead* against cancelling the rehearsal.
5. as modifiers of noun phrases: quite, rather, such	He is *quite* a handsome man. His flat was in *rather* a mess. She is *such* a funny woman.
6. as modifiers of nouns: (before or after the noun)	the example *below*; the day *before*; the interview *yesterday*; our neighbour *upstairs*; the years *ahead*; the *above* statement.

(c) *Adverbs as Complements of Prepositions*. Some adverbs act as complements of prepositions although this is a less common function compared with the two main functions above:

| Adverbs of Time | The bell rings *at noon*.
I haven't smoked *since March*. |

Adverbs of Place and Direction	George lives *in the country*. She called to me *from outside*.
Adverbs of Manner, etc.	Rowland left *in an angry mood*. She fits *in easily* with the group.
Adverbs of Degree	The rope is short *by two metres*.

Note: It is mostly Place and Time Adverbs which act as complements of prepositions.

D. *Positions of Adverbs*

Although it is possible for an adverb or an adverbial word group to occupy **initial position**, **mid-position** with the verb, or **final position**, all three positions are not always possible for each different type of adverb. The more common positions for the different types of adverbs are as follows:

Adverbs of Time 1. Definite time	usually final position but also: mid-position initial position	The ship will arrive *tomorrow*. I've *just* finished my work. *Now* he's living in Australia.
2. Duration/ Length of time	usually final position but also: mid-position	She's stopping work *temporarily*. He is *temporarily* out of work.
3. Frequency: – definite	usually final position	Public meetings take place *monthly*. I go to my office *every day*.
– indefinite	usually mid-position	She *generally* goes to bed at 10 o'clock. They *regularly* go to the swimming-pool.
Adverbs of Place and Direction	usually final position but also: initial position	It's cold *outside*. *Outside*, it was very hot.
Adverbs of Manner, Means & Instrument	usually final position but also: mid-position initial position	She dances very *gracefully*. She *quickly* left the room. *Quickly*, he took out his gun and fired.
Adverbs of Degree	usually mid-position but also: final position	I *completely* agreed with him. He ignored my request *completely*.

Conjunctive Adverbs	usually initial position or mid-position but also: final position	The motor you sent is defective; *therefore*, we are returning it to you. ...; we are *therefore* returning.... ...; we are returning it to you, *therefore*.
Sentence Adverbs	usually initial position but also: mid-position final position	*Fortunately*, no one was injured. ...; no one, *fortunately*, was injured. ...; no one was injured, *fortunately*.

Notes on Adverb Position

1. Intensifiers appear directly before the words they modify:

   It is *very/quite/rather/extremely* hot outside.

2. The position of an adverb in mid-position with the verb varies according to the number of auxiliaries that accompany the verb. An important rule to remember about an adverb in mid-position is that it is generally not placed between the verb and its object.

	Usual Position of Adverbs	*Examples*
(a) Verbs with no auxiliaries: (i) the verb *be* (ii) all other verbs (b) Verbs with one to three auxiliaries	after the verb before the verb after the first auxiliary	She is *sometimes* late. She *sometimes* comes late. She has *sometimes* come late. She has *sometimes* been coming late.

3. Two or more adverbials in mid-position:

   He is *now rapidly* approaching retirement age.
   He will *surely* be *severely* punished.

   The second adverb, which is usually an adverb of manner, is placed closest to the main part of the verb.

4. Adverbials in final position (i.e. an adverb or an adverbial word group used in final position after the verb and any complement(s) it may have). If more than one adverbial occurs in final position, the usual order is place, manner, time:

51

Subject	Verb + Complement	Place	Manner (also: Degree; Instrument; Purpose; Agent; Accompaniment)	Time: Frequency	Time: Duration, Definite Time
1	2	3	4	5	6
I	like him		more and more (degree)	each time I meet him.	
She	cut the meat		slowly. (manner) with a blunt knife. (instrument)		
She	was walking	along the road	quietly (manner) with her dog (accompaniment)		last night.
I	hope to go	to Bali	for a holiday (purpose)		next year.
This model aeroplane	can be made	at home	by young children. (agent) very easily. (manner) with a few simple tools. (instrument)		
Mrs Lee	visited her husband	in the hospital		every day	for a month. last year.

There is, in fact, a certain amount of flexibility in the sequence of adverbials in final position. A general rule is that a shorter adverbial precedes a longer one. However, a one-word adverbial like **here**, **there**, **away**, usually remains closest to the verb, and an adverbial of definite time like **today**, **yesterday**, **next month**, generally comes last.

5. Distribution of Adverbials. When several adverbials are used in a sentence, the tendency is to distribute them among the various positions that are natural to them, e.g.

> *Every day* he *eagerly* checked the crossword puzzle results.
> *Before* you come to dinner, put away your toys *quickly* and wash your hands *thoroughly*.

52

6. Reversal of word order after certain adverbials. The subject and verb are often reversed after:
(a) initial negatives:

Never	have	I	seen	such a sight.
Seldom	did	they	have	enough to eat.
No sooner	had	he	left	than the phone rang.

(b) initial 'only', 'so', 'such':

Only once	did	she	complain about her job.
So rapidly	did	the fire	spread that it was impossible to control.
Such rare orchids	as	they	are difficult to find.

(c) initial expressions of place:

There	stood	the tallest man he had ever seen.
Before them	lay	a large, shiny stone.
Inside the room	were	a few pieces of furniture.
On the desk	was	a pile of books.

Such a reversal, which allows more emphasis to be placed on the adverbial in initial position, often represents formal usage.

E. *Comparison of Adverbs*
1. Adverbs have the same general rules of comparison as adjectives (see page 44).

	Positive	Comparative	Superlative
Adjective	short	short*er*	short*est*
	beautiful	*more* beautiful	*most* beautiful
Adverb	soon	soon*er*	soon*est*
	clearly	*more* clearly	*most* clearly

2. The same rules of comparison for adjectives that are identical in form with adverbs, also apply:

early	earlier	earliest

53

3. As with adjectives, there is a small group of adverbs with irregular comparison:

badly	worse	worst
far	further/farther	furthest/farthest
little	less	least
much	more	most
well	better	best

4. Note that adverbs of two syllables ending in *-ly* do not follow the rule of adjectives ending in *-y* (e.g. funny, funnier, funniest). Instead they keep the *-ly* form:

slowly	more slowly	most slowly

Minor Word Classes

1. Auxiliary Verbs

A. *Types of Auxiliary Verbs*
1. Auxiliary verbs are commonly called 'helping verbs' because they are always followed by a main verb in a verb phrase. By themselves they cannot form a verb phrase.
2. There are two types of auxiliaries: **Primary Auxiliary Verbs** and **Modal Auxiliary Verbs**. The two types are illustrated in the table below:

Main Verbs	Auxiliary Verbs	
	Primary	*Modal*
run, frighten, jump, hate, love, write, look, draw, threaten, etc.	do have be	can, may, shall, will, could, might, should, would, used to, must, ought to, need, dare.

3. The auxiliaries are primarily used in the formation of the various tenses and aspects, for example:

be	+	*-ing* present participle for progressive forms	They *are writing* in their exercise books.
be	+	*-ed* past participle for passive forms	Thousands of people *were injured* in the earthquake.
have	+	*-ed* past participle for the perfect tenses	He *has* just *arrived*.
shall-will	+	simple form of the verb for the future tense	She *will come* at 10 a.m.

See pages 56-65 for further details of individual auxiliaries.

4. It is necessary to use auxiliary verbs in the formation of both questions and negatives:

> Questions: *Can* he speak French?
> *Will* you come to my house this evening?
> *Should* I wear a dress or a pair of jeans?

Notice that in the formation of questions, the auxiliary comes before the subject.

> Negatives: I *cannot/can't* hear you very well.
> They *are not/aren't* going away until Friday.
> He *might not/mightn't* be able to meet you until 5 o'clock.

Here the auxiliary verb comes before the negative *not*. The contracted (or shortened) negative forms are mostly found in spoken, informal English.

5. Positive contractions with auxiliaries. An auxiliary may contract not only with the negative *not* that follows it (see 4. above), but also with the subject that precedes it. These positive contractions with the subject take the following form:

be			*have*			*shall-will*		
am	—	*'m*	has	—	*'s*	shall-will	—	*'ll*
is	—	*'s*	have	—	*'ve*	should-would	—	*'d*
are	—	*'re*	had	—	*'d*			

Contractions with subjects do not occur with the primary auxiliary *do* or with modal auxiliaries. With the above auxiliaries they are usually used after:

(i) a pronoun	I *'m* going home.
	What *'ll* you do?
	He *'s* here already.
(ii) a short noun	My pen *'s* lost.
	The food *'ll* be cold.
(iii) the words *here*, *there* and *now*	Here *'s* your door key.
	Now *'s* the time.
	There *'ll* be a magician at the party.

55

6. Auxiliary verbs can be used without main verbs but only where the main verb is 'understood':

> I can swim as fast as she *can* (swim).

7. Verb phrases can contain up to three auxiliaries depending on the tense or aspect being used. It is important to note the correct sequence if more than one auxiliary is being used. See the table on page 39 for the use of more than one auxiliary with the passive.

B. *The Primary Auxiliaries* (do, have, be)

Do

1. Note the following forms of the auxiliary **do**:

Tense	Non-negative	Uncontracted Negative	Contracted Negative
Present: all persons singular and plural except 3rd person singular	do	do not	don't
	does	does not	doesn't
Past: all persons	did	did not	didn't
-ing form: (present participle) all persons	doing		
Past Participle: all persons	done	not done	

2. **Do** performs many functions:
   (i) as a main verb with the meaning of 'perform':

> I *do* my homework every night.
> She *does* her washing in the evenings.

   (ii) as a substitute verb; i.e. **do** can act as a substitute for the whole of a clause:

> I can speak French as well as he *does*. (= as he speaks French)

> A: Who wants to come with me to town?
> B: I *do* (n't).

> A: Have you sent your Christmas cards off yet?
> B: Yes, I *did* yesterday. (= I sent my cards off yesterday.)

   (iii) as a 'dummy' operator in the **do-** construction. When a verb phrase contains no auxiliary verbs, it therefore contains no

56

word that can act as operator for the purpose of forming **yes-no** questions and negative sentences with **not**:

> I *like* mangoes.
> He *needs* a haircut.
> Jill *fainted* yesterday.

For such verbs, a 'dummy' operator has to be introduced for (a) forming questions, and (b) *not* negation:

> (a) *Do* you *like* mangoes?   (b) I *don't like* mangoes.
>   *Does* he *need* a haircut?   He *doesn't need* a haircut.
>   *Did* Jill *faint* yesterday?   Jill *didn't faint* yesterday.

3. The auxiliary **do** has the full range of tense forms like other main verbs, including (a) the present participle **doing**, and (b) the past participle **done**:

> (a) What have you been *doing* all weekend?
> (b) I have *done* all the exercises in my Science Book.

Note however, that the auxiliary **do** is primarily used in (a) the simple present tense, and (b) the simple past tense:

> (a) I *do like* to go to the beach.
>   He *does try* to mend his own shirts.
> (b) I *did offer* to give him a lift.
>   He *did come* to my house yesterday.

Have

1. Note the following forms of the auxiliary **have**:

Tense	Uncontracted Non-negative	Contracted Non-negative	Uncontracted Negative	Contracted Negative
Present: all persons singular and plural except 3rd person singular	have	've	have not, 've not	haven't
	has	's	has not,	hasn't
Past Tense:	had	'd	had not, 'd not	hadn't
-ing form:	having		not having	
Past Participle:	had			

57

2. **Have** has the following functions:
   (i) as a main verb meaning 'possess':

   I *have* a new antique cupboard
   I *have* hundreds of paperback novels.
   or 'receive, take, experience':
   I *have* coffee and toast for breakfast.
   I *have* free time on the week-ends.

   (ii) The *do-* construction is used for interrogative and negative sentences with **have** as a main verb:

   Do you *have* much jewellery?
   Does he *have* sugar in his coffee?
   Did you *have* a good time last night?

   (iii) The auxiliary **have** is used to form the perfect aspect; i.e. a form of **have** is followed by a verb in the past participle form:

The present perfect	I *have baked* several cakes for my friends.
	She *has baked* several cakes for her friends.

The present perfect progressive	I *have been baking* cakes all morning.
	She *has been baking* cakes all morning.

The past perfect	I *had baked* three cakes by midday.
	She *had baked* three cakes by midday.

The past perfect progressive	I *had been baking* cakes all morning and felt hot and tired.
	She *had been baking* cakes all morning and felt hot and tired.

   (iv) In the construction of **have** + *to-* infinitive, only the finite (present and past) forms of **have** can be used:

   She *has to* look after her baby sister.
   They *have to* sit for their written test on Monday.
   I *had to* repeat my question.

Note that in such constructions, **have/has/had to-** carries the same meaning of necessity as **must**.

58

Be

1. The auxiliary **be** has eight different forms: **be, am, is, are, was, were, being, been**.

Tense	Non-negative	Uncontracted Negative	Contracted Negative
Base Form	be		
Present Tense: 1st person singular 2nd person singular 3rd person singular	am, 'm are, 're is, 's	am not, 'm not are not, 're not is not, 's not	*aren't, aren't isn't
1st person plural 2nd person plural 3rd person plural	are, 're	are not, 're not	aren't
Past Tense: 1st person singular 2nd person singular 3rd person singular	was were was	was not were not was not	wasn't weren't wasn't
1st person plural 2nd person plural 3rd person plural	were	were not	weren't
-ing form: (present participle)	being	not being	
-ed form: (past participle)	been		

*The *-nt* form for the 1st person singular is *aren't* and is only used in the phrase *Aren't I*?

59

2. **Be** is constructed as an auxiliary even when it functions as a main verb:

> I *am* a girl/ He *is* a boy.

3. It normally has no *do-* constructions unlike *have*, although the main verb **be** may have the *do-* construction in (a) imperative sentences, and (b) negative imperatives:

> (a) *Do be* quiet!
> (b) *Don't be* silly!

4. In the construction of **be** + *to-* infinitive, only the finite (present and past) forms of **be** can be used:

> The motor rally *is to start* tomorrow.

> not   †The motor rally $\left\{ \begin{array}{l} \text{will be} \\ \text{is being} \end{array} \right.$ to start tomorrow.

5. The main function of the auxiliary **be** is in the construction of:
   (a) the progressive aspect (**be** + *-ing* **present participle**)
       He *is opening* the exhibition now.
   (b) the passive (**be** + *-ed* **past participle**) (see page 39)
       Many students *were injured* in the clash.

C. *The Modal Auxiliaries*

1. Modal auxiliaries help to add a variety of special meanings (such as ability, permission, possibility, etc.) to the meaning of the main part of the verb.
2. They do not have *-s* forms, *-ing* forms, or *-ed* participles.
3. **Can, may, shall** and **will** have special past forms, but the rest of the modal auxiliaries do not.
4. Note the forms of the various modals:

Non-negative (all persons)	*Uncontracted Negative*	*Contracted Negative*
can	cannot, can not	can't
could	could not	couldn't
may	may not	mayn't
might	might not	mightn't
shall	shall not	shan't
should	should not	shouldn't
will, 'll	will not ('ll not)	won't
would, 'd	would not ('d not)	wouldn't

†non-standard

60

Non-negative (all persons)	Uncontracted Negative	Contracted Negative
must	must not	musn't
ought to	ought not to	oughtn't to
used to	used not to	didn't use(d) to
		usedn't to
need	need not	needn't
dare	dare not	daren't

Note:
1. **Mayn't** is rarely used, and is mostly used in British English.
2. **Shan't** is rare in American English.
3. **Ought** usually has the *to-* infinitive in questions and negative sentences, but occasionally the bare infinitive is used:
   to- infinitive: You *oughtn't to* drink so much.
   bare infinitive: You *oughtn't* drink so much.
4. **Used to** always takes the *to-* infinitive and occurs only in the past tense. It may take the *do-* construction with *used to*:

   She *didn't use(d) to* smoke so much.
   Did he *use(d) to* work for your father?

5. **Dare** and **Need** can be constructed in two ways:
   (i) as modal auxiliaries (with bare infinitive and without the inflected forms dares/needs; dared/needed); or
   (ii) as main verbs (with *to-* infinitive, *-s* inflection and past forms).
   Dare and **Need** as auxiliaries are mainly used with negative and interrogative sentences, whereas as main verbs they can be used in all forms:

Need	as a Modal Auxiliary	as a Main Verb
positive		She *needs* to wash her hair.
negative	She *needn't* wash her hair.	She *doesn't need* to wash her hair.
interrogative	*Need* she wash her hair?	*Does* she *need* to wash her hair?
negative-interrogative	*Needn't* she wash her hair?	*Doesn't* she *need* to wash her hair?

61

6. As with the auxiliary verb *do*, other auxiliaries can act as a substitute for a whole or part of a sentence following the auxiliary:

> She *can* mend a puncture as well as he *can*. (= mend a puncture)
> I*'ll* go to dancing classes if you *will*. (= go to dancing classes, too)

> A: He *is* working hard on his model boat.
> B: Yes, he *is*. (= working hard on his model boat)

> You *can* write in this workbook but you *mustn't* (= write) in that text.

> A: Did you lock the house?
> B: No, but I *should have*. (= locked the house)

D. *Special Meanings of Modal Auxiliaries*
Below are examples of some of the special meanings of the various modal auxiliaries:

Can (past *Could*)

Physical ability	*Can* you reach the top shelf? I *can* lift that box by myself.
Learned ability	She *can* type. *Can* you drive a car? He *could* read when he was three years old.
Have the power to	This factory *can* produce dozens of cars a day. This error *can* be corrected easily.
Requesting permission (informal)	*Can* I borrow your car? I wonder if I *could* speak to you for a while.
Possibility:—in theory —tentative possibility	The roads *can* be improved. He *could* have left his car keys in his office.
Can = 'sometimes'	Electrical storms *can* be dangerous.
Could = suggestion	You *could* peel those potatoes for me.
Could = permission in the past	When I was at university, I *could* get cheap air fares.
Can't = prohibition or negation of permission	You *can't* go swimming today.

62

May (past *Might*)	
Requesting permission (formal/polite)	*May* I see you tonight? *Might* I borrow your car? You *might* find the book in the library.
Possibility	The monsoon rains *may* damage the padi harvest. The missing child *might* have been kidnapped.
Suggestion (polite)	*Might* I suggest that we continue our discussion another day? You *might* check the errors in this paper.
May not = 'can't'/prohibition	You *may not* stay out until midnight.
Shall (past *Should*)	
Probability/expectation	The train *should* be here any moment. They *should* be home by now.
Improbability (negative form)	There *shouldn't* be any trouble.
Obligation:— insistence (restricted to formal documents and regulations)	Nine people *shall* be elected to the committee.
— which may not be fulfilled	You *should* hand in your essays next Friday.
Suggestion	*Shall* we go and see a film?
Advisability	She *should* eat less if she wants to lose weight. You *should* stay in bed if you're unwell.
Prohibition (negative advice)	You *shouldn't* be so rude. I *shouldn't* have left the door unlocked.
Will (past *Would*)	
Willingness	The maid *will* help you with your bags. Who *will* lend me five dollars until tomorrow?

Prediction	Faisal *will* have arrived in New York by now.
Predictability	A dog *will* attack a child if it is teased. He *will* lose his hand if it gets caught in that machine.
Requests	*Will* you take my coat to the cleaners? *Would* you carry this upstairs for me?
Invitations	*Would* you like to come with me to town? How *would* you like to come to Penang with my family? *Will* you be free to come to dinner tomorrow night?
Offers	*Would* you like another glass of wine?
Refusal (negative forms)	She *won't* follow my advice. They *wouldn't* come over for supper.
Promise	I promise I *won't* (will not) ask for money again. I*'ll* give you the book as soon as I've read it.
Must (= have to) Certainty (about an event)	There *must* be some mistake. I *must* leave right away.
Inference (about an event in the past or present)	There *must* be a fire near by. There *must* have been a thousand people at the wedding.
Obligation/compulsion	You *must* be back by three o'clock. He *must* return the money immediately.
Mustn't = prohibition (negation of permission)	You *mustn't* smoke in here.
Advice not to do something	You *mustn't* keep your mother waiting.
Ought to (= should) Probability	My friend *ought* to be here soon.

64

Obligation (which may not be fulfilled)	I *ought* to go to the library tonight (but I probably won't). You *ought* to do your homework every day.
Prohibition (= negative advice)	You *oughtn't* spend so much time on the golf course.
Advice	You *ought* to clean the air-conditioner at least once a year. Everyone *ought* to go to the dentist every six months.

Used to

Past habit or custom	He *used* to play tennis very often but now he's too busy. We *used* to eat meat every day when it was cheaper.

Need

Need = 'must' (in questions and negatives) i.e. obligation and necessity	*Need* he have a reason for marrying her? Does he *need* to attend the orientation programme?
Lack of necessity/compulsion	She *need* not worry about her grades. They *needn't* go to the lecture hall yet.

Dare

Threat/Warning	Don't you *dare* slam the door in my face! Don't you *dare* talk about my sister like that!
Dare = 'have the courage'	No soldier *dare* disobey his commanding officer. I wouldn't *dare* enter his room without permission.

2. Determiners

1. The term **determiner** covers several classes of words which, in older grammar books and dictionaries are called pronouns or adjectives. It includes the definite and indefinite articles, the demonstratives and adjectives of indefinite number and quantity, numerals and possessives.

2. Determiners are words which identify or specify a noun in various ways, e.g. by making it definite (*the* child), indefinite (*a* child), or by indicating quantity or amount (*many/three/some* children; *some/no/a little* water).

3. For the purpose of setting out which determiners are used (or not used) with nouns, we have to understand the difference between count nouns, plural count nouns and uncountables (see page 9).

4. Determiners always precede the noun they determine though, if more than one determiner is used, we need to consider the rules regarding their positions.

5. Determiners can be categorized into three types: Predeterminers, Determiners themselves and Postdeterminers. The Determiners themselves comprise the most important category and they can be preceded by predeterminers and/or followed by postdeterminers. All three types can be preceded by intensifiers of the entire noun phrase:

Sequence of Determiners			
Intensifiers (adverbs) 1	*Predeterminers* 2	*Determiners* 3	*Postdeterminers* 4
even only just	1. both, all, half 2. *Multipliers*: once, twice, double, triple, many times, ten times, etc. 3. *Fractions*: a quarter, two-thirds, etc. 4. what, such, quite, rather	1. *Articles*: a(n), the 2. *Demonstratives*: this, that, those, these 3. *Possessives*: my, yours, his 4. *Quantifiers*: some, any, each, every, no, either, neither 5. *Wh- determiners*: what(ever), who-(ever), whose, which(ever), etc.	1. *Cardinal Numbers*: one, two, three, etc. 2. *Ordinal Numbers*: first, second, third, etc. 3. *General Ordinals*: other, more, next, last, following 4. *Quantifiers*: many, few, several, little, more, less, etc.

A. Determiners

(a) Articles: (a(n), the)

1. English has two articles, the **definite article** and the **indefinite article**. Sometimes a noun does not require an article.
2. The definite article **(the)** can be used with all types of noun except most proper nouns.
3. In contrast, the indefinite article can normally only be used with singular count nouns.
4. **Some** is used for indefinite meaning with plural count nouns and mass nouns that cannot take the indefinite article:

	The Definite Article (for definite meaning)	The Indefinite Article (for indefinite meaning)
Singular count nouns	the house/car	a house/car
Plural count nouns	the houses/cars	(some) houses/cars
(Singular) mass nouns	the bread	(some) bread

5. Certain common nouns do not take any articles, especially when they are used in idiomatic expressions. In other contexts they may take an article:

With an article		Without an article
Transport:		
ride on *a* bicycle		by bicycle
sit in *a* taxi	come	by bus
catch *the* plane	leave	by boat/ship
drive *the* car	travel	by train
Places/Institutions:		
walk into *the* hotel/prison/club		bed
drive to *the* school/station	be in	church
lie on *the* bed	go to	prison
		hospital
		be at school/university/college
		go to sea
		be in town, go home, leave home

Times:
in *the* morning/evening
during *the* day/night
at *the* stroke of midnight

They met
- at dawn.
- at daybreak.
- at sunrise.
- at sunset.
- at noon.
- at midday.
- at midnight.
- at dusk.
- at night.

Meals:
Have you cooked *the* lunch/dinner?
Did you attend *the* dinner for . . .?

I'll
- have
- stay for
- come for

He came
- before
- at
- after
- during

- breakfast.
- dinner.
- tea.
- lunch.
- supper.

(b) *Demonstratives:* (this, that, these, those)

The four demonstratives—two expressing 'nearness' **(this, these)** and the two expressing 'distance' **(that, those)**—act as determiners in such sentences as:

I like
- *this flower/these flowers.*
- *that flower/those flowers.*

They are used with singular count nouns, plural count nouns and mass nouns:

Can you post *this letter*?
I can't fit into *these blouses* anymore.
I found *that (newspaper) article* very difficult to understand.

(c) *Possessives:* (my, your, his, etc.)

There are two kinds of possessives—determiners and pronouns (see page 74). Each has a different function. The English language uses determiner-type possessives with reference to personal belongings and parts of the body:

my
your
his
} leg/arm/teeth/feet/hair/ankle

$$\left.\begin{array}{l}\text{my} \\ \text{your} \\ \text{his}\end{array}\right\} \text{car/house/pen/screwdriver/magazine}$$

Possessives as determiners are used in a central position with all types of noun (singular or plural count and mass nouns):

I have lost *my* handbag/*my* keys/*my* money.

(d) *Quantifiers:* (some, any, no, every, each, either, enough, etc.)

Like possessives, quantifiers have more than one function—as determiners and as pronouns. As determiners, quantifiers may function also in a predeterminer and postdeterminer position.

Quantifier Determiners			
Types of Quantifier Determiners	Count		Mass Singular
	Singular	Plural	
1. quantifiers with 'inclusive' meaning	all every each — half	all — — both half	all — — — half
2. *some* and *any* words	some any either neither	some any — —	some any — —
3. quantifiers expressing degree of quantity/ amount	— — — — — — — —	many more most enough (a) few fewer/less fewest several	much more most enough (a) little less least
4. indefinite quantifiers	one	—	—
5. negative quantifiers	no neither	no —	no —

Examples of the different types of quantifier determiners (in all positions):

1. She gave sweets/money to *all* the children.
   He cleaned *both* cars.

69

She gave *half* the orange/oranges/bread to her sister.
Give a song book to *every/each* child.

2. I did come across *some* book on that topic in the library.
She found *some* cheese/eggs in the refrigerator.
Did *any* tables/furniture get burnt?
Either method will work.

3. Did you notice $\left\{ \begin{array}{l} \textit{many} \text{ chairs} \\ \textit{much} \text{ furniture} \end{array} \right\}$ in the room?

There $\left\{ \begin{array}{l} \text{are } \textit{more} \text{ potatoes} \\ \text{is } \textit{more} \text{ rice} \end{array} \right\}$ if you're still hungry.

Have you got *enough* spices/pepper for the curry?

The chairman $\left\{ \begin{array}{l} \text{has } \textit{little} \text{ assistance from} \\ \text{has } \textit{few} \text{ assistants in} \end{array} \right\}$ his committee.

She has been fasting for *several* days.

4. I'll come and visit you *one* day.

5. He has *no* trouble with his work.
She has *no* problems to sort out.

(e) *Wh- Determiners:* (what(ever), which(ever), who(ever), whose)

Wh- determiners are interrogatives which introduce *wh-* questions. They belong to the same *wh-* words as relative pronouns. However, their function is different. As determiners, *wh-* words precede the noun in noun phrases and refer to:

(a) both personal and non-personal nouns (i.e. masculine, feminine and neutral nouns) (= common and neuter);

(b) all classes of nouns (count singular and plural, and mass);

(c) definite and indefinite things and people:

> *What* pop singer do you like best?
> *Which* pop singer do you prefer?
> *Whose* pen/pencils/ink did you borrow?
> *Whose* children are they?
> *What* magazines did you buy?
> *Which* magazines do you like best?
> *Whose* paperback is this?
> You can call me *whatever* names you like.
> You should buy *whichever* dress you like best.

B. *Predeterminers*

Predeterminers, when combined with determiners, occur before them. There are four types of predeterminers:

70

(a) *all, both, half*:

These determiners occur with the following nouns:

	Count Singular	Count Plural	Mass	
all		✓	✓	Can you eat *all those apples*? Can you eat *all that rice*?
both		✓		*Both of his sisters* are tall.
half	✓	✓	✓	*Half (of) the apple* was bad. *Half (of) these apples* are rotten. He spends *half his time* in France.

All, **both** and **half** as predeterminers come before articles (*both the* girls), possessives (*all my* friends), or demonstratives (*half those* apples). Because predeterminers themselves denote quantity they cannot occur with other quantifiers such as **any**, **some**, **enough**, **each**.

Note that **both**, **all** and **half** may also be followed by **of** as the sentences above show.

(b) *Multipliers:* (once, twice, three times, etc.)

These occur with singular and plural count nouns or mass nouns expressing amount and degree:

> He has *twice the strength* of most boys his age.
> The dinner is going to cost *two times the amount* we had budgeted for.
> They want the Ministry to give them *double their current allowance*.

These determiners can occur with **a**, **every**, **each** to form frequency adverbials:

I see my boyfriend	once	a	day.
	twice	every	week.
	three times	each	month.

(c) *Fractions:* (a quarter, two-thirds, etc.)

These can be followed by determiners. The *of-* construction is optional:

> He completed the Big Walk in *a quarter (of) the time* I did.
> He scored *two-thirds of the total possible marks*.

71

(d) *What, such, rather, quite:*

These degree determiners function as modifiers of noun phrases. They occur:

(a) before the indefinite article with singular count nouns;

(b) without an article with plural count nouns and mass nouns:

> *What a pity*!
> It was *such a pity*!
> There was *quite a large crowd*.
> It was *rather a long way*.
> What $\begin{Bmatrix} \textit{healthy plants} \\ \textit{attractive furniture} \end{Bmatrix}$ you have!
> They were *such interesting people*.
> We had *such hot weather* in February.

C. *Postdeterminers*

Postdeterminers can follow any determiners but they must occur before nouns, participles and adjectives. There are three types:

(a) *Cardinal Numbers:* (one, two, four, etc.)

One, naturally, can only occur with singular count nouns but all other cardinal numbers occur only with plural count nouns:

> I have *one nose* and *two ears*.

(b) *Ordinal Numbers:* (first, second, third, etc.)

These occur only with count nouns. They usually come before any cardinal numbers in a noun phrase although this depends on the context:

> He won *first prize*.
> usually ⎰ The *first five places* were awarded to 'B' House.
> but   ⎱ She won *two first prizes* in the contest.

(c) *General Ordinals*: (next, last, (an)other, further, etc.)

These may either precede or follow the ordinal numbers:

> His *last two novels* were bestsellers.
> The *other three candidates* were women.
> There were *four other people* in the taxi.
> There are *five further chapters* to read.

72

(d) *Quantifiers:* (many, a few, fewer, several, much, etc.)

Quantifiers as postdeterminers are usually those that express degrees of quantity/amount (see page 69). Examples:

1. **Many, (a) few, fewer, several:**

   These occur only with plural count nouns. Note that **several** is hardly ever preceded by a determiner.

   > *Her many relatives* visit very often.
   > There were *very few bargains* left at the sale.
   > The headmaster wanted to have *a few words* with the staff.
   > *Several eggs* were thrown at the speaker.

2. **Much** and **(a) little** occur only with mass nouns:

   > We have *a little time* to spare before our guests arrive.
   > There isn't *much tea* in the tin.

3. **More** occurs with plural and mass nouns, and **less** usually only with mass nouns:

   > We have *some more* $\left\{ \begin{array}{c} books \\ paper \end{array} \right\}$ in the store room.
   > Please make *less noise* in the library!

4. Phrases can also denote quantity, occurring with both plural count nouns and mass nouns:

   > The safe contains $\left\{ \begin{array}{l} plenty\ of \\ a\ lot\ of \\ lots\ of \end{array} \right\}$ documents/money.

5. Quantifying phrases with numbers are used only with count nouns in the plural:

   > The safe contained $\left\{ \begin{array}{l} a\ (great) \\ a\ (large) \\ a\ (good) \end{array} \right\}$ *number of* documents/files.

6. Phrases with **deal** and **amount** can only be used with mass nouns:

   > The safe contained $\left\{ \begin{array}{l} a\ great \\ a\ good \\ a\ large \\ a\ small \end{array} \right\} \left\{ \begin{array}{l} deal\ of \\ \\ amount\ of \end{array} \right\}$ money.

3. Pronouns

A. *General Functions of Pronouns*

1. Pronouns are words that are used in place of a noun or noun phrase; that is, they can function as the subject or object of a clause, often acting as substitutes for noun phrases. Generally though, pronouns function as a whole noun phrase without the need for determiners or modifiers.

> *Laila* has lost *her* handbag.
> *Mr Moore* is here to see you. Shall I show *him* in?
> Could you mend this *dress*? *It* has a button off the front.
> *The students* have already submitted *their assignments*. *They* say *they* gave *them* to *their* group leader.
> *She* cut *herself*.
> Can you lend me *a few plates*? I need *some*.
> *You* and *I* ought to rent *our* car to them.

2. One of the problems in dealing with pronouns is that they are often related to other word classes with the same word acting as a pronoun in one context and as another item in another context. For example, many items can function both as determiners (which require a headword) and as pronouns (which do not require a headword). Others can be determiners only, or pronouns only:

As Determiners (+ headword)	*As Pronoun* (no headword)
Which house is hers?	*Which* is hers?
This car is mine.	*This* is my car.
Inform me of *whatever decision* you arrive at.	Take *whatever* you want.

As Determiner only	*As Pronoun only*
The watch is mine.	We spoke to the prisoners *themselves*.

B. *Kinds of Pronouns*

Personal and Reflexive Pronouns

Personal and reflexive pronouns have three characteristics in common:

1. They distinguish between masculine and feminine within personal **gender**, and neutral (non-personal) **gender**:

personal	{	masculine	he	himself
	{	feminine	she	herself
neutral (non-personal)			it	itself

74

2. They distinguish between first, second and third **person**:

first	I, we	myself, ourselves
second	you	yourself, yourselves
third	he, she, it, they	himself, herself, itself, themselves

3. They distinguish between singular and plural **number**:

singular	I, he, she, it	myself, himself, etc.
plural	we, they	ourselves, themselves

Number		Gender	*Personal Pronouns*		*Possessives*		*Reflexive Pronouns*
			Subjective Case (i.e. acting as subject)	*Objective Case (i.e. acting as object)*	*Possessive Determiners*	*Possessive Pronouns*	
1st person	singular		I	me	my	mine	myself
	plural		we	us	our	ours	ourselves
2nd person	singular		you		your	yours	yourself
	plural						yourselves
3rd person	singular	masculine	he	him	his		himself
		feminine	she	her	her	hers	herself
		neutral	it		its		itself
	plural		they	them	their	theirs	themselves

PERSONAL, POSSESSIVE, AND REFLEXIVE PRONOUNS

(a) *Personal Pronouns*
1. Personal pronouns are classified according to person (1st, 2nd and 3rd person), number (singular, plural), gender (masculine, feminine, neutral), and case (subjective (nominative in older grammar books), objective and genetive).
2. Five personal pronouns have both **subjective** and **objective** case forms as well as two **genetive case** forms (known as 'Possessives'). See table above. This means that, unlike nouns which retain the

same form regardless of where they are used in a sentence, these five pronouns change their form to indicate how they are used.

3. The choice of person, number, and gender of personal pronouns also depends on the meaning of the sentence or on the noun phrase the noun is replacing. This means that pronouns must **agree** in number, gender and person with the word for which a pronoun stands (i.e. the antecedent):

(i) **Number:**

Every *girl* must bring *her* swimsuit.
Nobody forgot *his* lunch.

Note: When the antecedent is a collective (group) noun, a singular pronoun is used if the members of the group act as a unit; a plural pronoun is used if they act separately:

The *class* held *its* election. (= unit)
The *class* gave *their* reports. (= individuals)

(ii) **Gender:**

Marie wore *her* hat; Ian wore *his*.
The tree shed *its* leaves.

Note: (a) If the antecedent may be considered either masculine or feminine, a masculine pronoun is used:

rather than   A child must learn to do *his* own work.
                A child must learn to do his or her own work.

(b) Generally speaking, **its** and not **his** is used in referring to an animal, except when it has a name;

The dog wagged *its* tail.
Fido wagged *his* tail.

(iii) **Person:**

Each *applicant* takes a test. Then *he* may be interviewed.

Similarly, a verb must agree with the pronoun used as its subject, in the same way a noun agrees with its subject (see page 14 for rules).

4. Generally, pronouns substitute a noun phrase which precedes them, though the pronoun can appear in other positions:

As soon as *the racing car* had refuelled, *it* started off again.
The racing car started off again as soon as *it* had refuelled.
As soon as *it* had refuelled, *the racing car* started off again.

76

5. Case Problems with Personal Pronouns. The choice of the subjective or objective case depends on the position of the pronoun in the sentence.

The **subjective form** is used in **subject position** with finite verbs:

> *We* were early for the film.

The **objective form** is used in **all other positions**: as direct objects, indirect objects or objects of prepositions:

> Their mother is taking *them* to the theatre. (= direct object)
> Mr Thomas gave *me* a job today. (= indirect object)
> No one came on time except *me*. (= object of preposition)

When a pronoun is part of a compound, the above case rules still apply:

> Alia and *I* will go. (= subject)
> Father sent Hew and *me* to the store. (= direct object)
> Mr Thomas gave Alex and *me* a job today. (= indirect object)
> No one came on time except Razli and *me*. (= object of preposition)

A help in many instances is to take out the other member of the compound. Then the choice is easy:

> Wait for Lily and (I, me). Wait for (I̶ me).

Again, with **we** or **us**, correct usage can be determined by omitting the noun and seeing which sounds better:

> (We, Us) boys were there. (We, U̶s̶) were there.

In making an incomplete comparison introduced by **than** or **an**, the comparison needs to be completed to decide whether a subjective, or an objective, pronoun is needed:

> She is taller than (I, me). She is taller than *I* am tall.
> I like Suzi as much as (her, she). I like Suzi as much as I like *her*.

(b) *Possessive Pronouns*

There are two kinds of possessives (see page 75). They can act:

1. as determiners:

My, our, your, his, hers, its, theirs act as determiners before noun heads:

> That is *my* bicycle.
> Give me *your* plate.

2. as pronouns:

Mine, ours, yours, his, hers, its, theirs act as pronouns in all main positions where a noun phrase is possible:

as subject	Let's go in my car. *Mine* (= my car) is faster.
as subject complement	Is this comic book *hers*? (= 'belong to her')
as object	He didn't bring a jacket, so I lent him *mine*. (= my jacket)
as prepositional complement	He put his books on the desk behind *mine*. (= my desk)
in comparison after *as*, *than*	Our car is older than *theirs*. (= their car) Our car is not as old as *theirs*.

Note:

1. No apostrophe is used after possessive pronouns.
2. Personal pronouns may appear in double possessive constructions beginning with **of**:

> He is a good friend *of mine*.
> Some students *of hers* were on a TV quiz programme.
> That car *of theirs* always gives them trouble.

(c) *Reflexive Pronouns*

A reflexive pronoun generally **points back to the subject**. It is used:

1. as the direct object of the verb:

> You mustn't blame *yourself* for that.
> Albert Schweitzer dedicated *himself* to caring for the sick in Africa.

2. as the indirect object of the verb:

> I bought *myself* a beautiful gold chain.
> She made *herself* a dress.

3. as a prepositional object:
   (a) of a verb:

> He's very selfish; he thinks only about *himself*.
> We should depend on *ourselves* rather than on others.

   (b) of an adjective:

> She's very angry with *herself* for making such a mistake.

4. as intensifiers (to emphasize nouns or pronouns):
   (a) intensifying a subject:

   We *ourselves* will lead the discussion.
   The party members *themselves* don't believe that their leaders are honest.
   The victims *themselves* can't explain how the accident happened.

   (b) intensifying an object:

   I saw the manager *himself*.
   We spoke to the victims *themselves*.
   The report was written by the department head *himself*.

(d) *Relative Pronouns*

1. The relative pronouns of English are **who, whom, whose, which, that,** and **zero,** i.e. a pronoun which is not pronounced but which can fill the position of a subject, object, etc. in a clause:

   with relative pronoun **which**: The cats *which he breeds* are mostly Siamese.
   with relative pronoun **zero** ϕ: The cats *he breeds* are mostly Siamese.

2. Types of Relative Pronouns

	Personal	*Neutral (Non-personal)*	*Personal and Neutral (Non-personal)*
subjective case	who	which	that
objective case	who(m)		that, ϕ (pronoun omitted)
genetive (possessive) case	whose	of which/ whose	

Wh- Pronouns

1. **Who, whom** and **whose** are used in a relative clause if the antecedent has a personal (masculine or feminine) gender:

   There's a woman at the door *who* wants to see you.
   Please let me know to *whom* the money should be sent.
   The girl *whose* mother you met, is the brightest student in the school.

79

Note: **Whose** can be used where the antecedent is neutral (non-personal) but generally **whose** is avoided in favour of the **of which** phrase:

> The car *whose* windscreen was broken has been fixed.
> The car, the windscreen *of which* was broken, has been fixed.

2. *Who* and *whom*. **Who** is used as the subject while **whom** is used as the object (direct object, indirect object or object of a preposition) in a relative clause:

> *Who* will offer to help us? ⎫
> *Who* is watering the plants? ⎬ (subject)
>
> *Whom* shall I send? (direct object)
> The man *whom* you want is the gardener. (indirect object)
> I know from *whom* he received the money. (object of preposition)

Note: In informal usage, **who** is often used as the object of a verb:

> *Who*(m) do you want?
> *Who*(m) are they discussing?
> I know the girl *who*(m) he's going to marry.

3. **Which** (and sometimes **whose**) is used if the antecedent has a non-personal (neutral) gender:

> I prefer a car *which* is economical to run.

That Pronoun

That is used to refer to both personal and non-personal antecedents. Note that it cannot follow a preposition (compared with **who** and **whom**) though it can be the object of a preposition. Thus, **that** has three functions:

1. as the subject of a relative clause:

> Do you know anyone *that* can repair this car?

2. as the object of a relative clause:

> Do you know the lecturer *that* we met?
> That's the boat *that* I've bought.

3. as the object of a preposition:

> Do you know the girl *that* your son writes *to*?
> This is the shop *that* I was talking *about*.

80

Zero Relative Pronoun (φ)

φ is used like **that** except that it cannot be the subject of a clause:

as object   Do you know the lecturer   { φ we met?
                                                     { that we met?

as subject   Do you know anyone   { †can repair this car?
                                                     { that can repair this car?

(e) *Interrogative Pronouns*

    The interrogative (*wh*−) words in English are **who, whom, whose, which, what, where, when, how, why, whether, if** (= whether). **Which** and **what** also function as determiners (see page 70). **Who, whom, whose, which** and **what** are also used as relative pronouns. As such they can and have both personal (masculine and feminine) and neutral (non-personal) reference as well as specific/general reference:

	Personal	*Neutral (Non-personal)*
subjective case	who what which	*what
objective case	who whom which	which
genetive (possessive) case	whose	

Examples:

1. Personal reference (referring to persons):

    Specific (definite)   *Who* is the best student in the form?
                                       Whom is he following?

    General (indefinite)   *Which* is the best speaker: Roberts
                                       or Hogan?

2. Neutral reference (not referring to persons):

    Specific (definite)   *What's* the title of your book?

    General (indefinite)   *Which* do you prefer: historical
                                       novels or biography?

    Note: **What**, when used for personal reference, is restricted to questions regarding jobs, professions, role, status, etc.:

        What's his occupation?

        What's your husband?   (= What is his job?)

†non-standard

(f) *Demonstrative Pronouns*

The demonstrative words in English are **this, that, these** and **those**. Like interrogatives, they can function both as determiners (see page 68) and as pronouns.

As pronouns they normally have neutral (non-personal) reference except when they are used in subject position:

as subject	*This* is my	husband. eldest son. new office. favourite dessert.
neutral (non-personal) reference		Do you want to buy *this* dress/ scarf/handbag, etc.? I found *these* vases/plates/spoons, etc. in an antique shop.

(g) *Quantifier Pronouns*

Quantifiers also function as both determiners (see page 69) and pronouns. As pronouns they may take an *of-* phrase. A comparison of the table below with the table on page 69, will show that the quantitative determiners **every** and **no** do not act as pronouns, but are replaced by **everyone** and **none**:

Quantifier Pronouns			
Types of Quantifiers as Pronouns with -of construction	Count Singular	Plural	Mass Singular
1. with 'inclusive' meaning	all (of) each (of) half (of)	all (of) both (of) half (of)	all (of) – half (of)
2. *some* and *any* words	some (of) any (of) either (of)	some (of) any (of) –	some (of) any (of) –
3. expressing degree of quantity/ amount	– – – – – – – –	many (of) more (of) most (of) enough (of) (a) few (of) fewer/less (of) fewest (of) several (of)	much (of) more (of) most (of) enough (of) (a) little (of) less (of) least (of) least (of)
4. indefinite quan- tifiers	one (of)	–	–
5. negative quantifiers	none (of) neither (of)	none (of) –	none (of) –

Functionally, the pronouns with the *of-* construction correspond closely to the function of the determiners:

Singular count pronouns: Can *any of you* take me to the station?
Would *each of you* bring some food for the picnic?
Can *either of you* tell me the time?

Plural count pronouns:

Have you read $\left\{\begin{array}{l}\text{any}\\ \text{some}\\ \text{most}\\ \text{many}\\ \text{a few}\\ \text{several}\\ \text{all}\end{array}\right\}$ of his short stories?

Singular mass pronouns:

Did you manage to get $\left\{\begin{array}{l}\text{a little}\\ \text{some}\\ \text{any}\\ \text{much}\end{array}\right\}$ of the chicken?

(h) *Other Quantifier Pronouns*

Other quantifier pronouns include singular pronouns which have either personal (masculine and feminine) or neutral (non-personal) reference:

	Personal	*Neutral (Non-personal)*
with 'inclusive' meaning	everybody, everyone	everything
some or *any* words	somebody, someone, anybody, anyone	something anything
negatives	nobody, no one	nothing

Examples:
Everyone/Everybody in the office is pleased with *everything* the new manager does.
Somebody/Someone is coming up the driveway.

A: Were you looking for *something*?
B: No, *nothing*.

A: Does *anybody/anyone* want to come with me to a film? *Nobody*?
B: I'll go with you if *nobody* else wants to. I've got *nothing* to do.

83

One. Although **one** is a numeral it can function as a pronoun in three ways:
1. in conjunction with other quantifiers, e.g. **every**, **each**, **any**:

> Every *one* of the children has measles.
> Each *one* of the old people was given a tin of biscuits.
> Any *one* of the candidates would be suitable.

2. as a substitute for a noun or noun phrase:

> I'd like to look at some drinking glasses, please. Have you any crystal *ones*?
> There are three books on orchids. Which *one* would you like?

3. to refer to people in general:

> *One* should always be careful when crossing the street.

Pronouns for General Statements. Other pronouns, apart from **one** above, may be used to represent people in general:

We	*We* all have sleepless nights sometimes.
	We all feel angry when the price of food continues to rise.
They	*They* say that the old wooden house over there is beautiful.
	They say that honesty is the best policy.
You	*You* have to study very hard at the university.
	You need to consider carefully before you buy a house.
Everybody/	*Everybody* should obey the traffic rules.
Everyone	*Everyone* should study more than one language at school.

In making general statements, it is important not to shift from one pronoun to another, but to keep using the same pronoun:

> *One* should do *one*'s (or his) duty in society.
> *We* all need to relax after *we* have worked hard all day.

84

(i) Reciprocal Pronouns

Each other and **one another** are reciprocal pronouns:

The twins always borrow clothes from $\begin{cases} \textit{each other.} \\ \textit{one another.} \end{cases}$

The boys in Form 5B are very loyal to $\begin{cases} \textit{each other,} \\ \textit{one another,} \end{cases}$

and they often borrow $\begin{cases} \textit{each other's} \\ \textit{one another's} \end{cases}$ books.

Pronouns with -ever

The *-ever* forms of pronouns—**whatever, whoever, whichever**—have several uses:

1. as intensifiers in questions:

   Whatever made you be so rude to that woman?
   Whoever told you such a story?

2. as intensifiers in negatives:

   I have no money *whatever*. (= at all)
   She doesn't speak any English *whatever*. (= at all)

3. as alternatives for **no matter who/which/what**:

   She complains about her mother-in-law to *whoever* she meets.
   Whoever comes to the house, don't let him in.

4. as introductory words in noun clauses:

   Borrow *whatever* you like.
   Whoever wrote on the desk must clean it off.

4. Prepositions

A. *Functions of Prepositions*

The function of prepositions is to connect a noun structure to some other word in a sentence. This noun structure may be:

1. a noun:	The salesman showed the pots and pans *to his wife*.
2. a pronoun:	The salesman showed the pots and pans *to her*.
3. a gerund phrase:	The salesman did not mind *showing the the pots and pans to her*.
4. a noun phrase:	The salesman showed the pots and pans *to whoever might want to buy them*.

Prepositions also have special functions as:
1. part of a verb (verb-preposition combinations):

> *look over* (= review); *get up* (= wake up)

2. an adverb (mostly adverbs of place and direction):

> They went *down*. ('down' = adverb)
> They went *down* the steps. ('down' = preposition)

B. *Forms of Prepositions*
Prepositions may consist of one, two or three parts:

1. *Examples of One-part prepositions*:

about	before	for	on	to
above	below	from	over	under
after	beside	in	past	until
along	between	into	since	up
around	by	of	till	with
at	down	off	through	without

2. *Examples of Two-part prepositions*:

according to	because of	out of
along with	due to	owing to
as for	except for	up to
away from		

3. *Examples of Three-part prepositions*:

by means of	in relation to
in comparison with	on top of
in front of	

C. *Positions of Prepositions*
Generally a preposition comes before its noun object:

> He gave the book *to the teacher*.

However, it may appear in final position in:
1. a question   Which school does he go *to*?
2. an adjective clause   There is the school that he goes *to*.
3. a noun clause   I don't know which school he goes *to*.

86

D. *Meanings of Prepositions*

Concepts of Time, Place, Direction and Distance, etc. can be expressed by prepositions. Such prepositions normally have an adverbial position in a sentence.

(a) *Prepositions of Time*

These can express:
1. one point in time:

    at — with *noon*, *night*, *midnight*; with the *time of day*.
2. periods of time:

    on — with *days*.

    in — with periods longer or shorter than a day; i.e. with *parts of the day*, with *months*, with *years*, with *seasons*.
3. extended time (duration):

    since, for, by, from ... to, from ... until, during, (with)in, while.

Examples:

They are getting married *on* Saturday *at* 4 o'clock *in* the evening.

The reception will be *on* Sunday *at* 3 o'clock *in* the afternoon.

He has been away from home *since* 16 March.

World War II lasted *from* 1939 *to/until* 1945.

He has not felt well *for* a long time, ever *since* his accident.

She has been away from school *for* two weeks.

I'll ring you again *within* the month.

Note:
1. **At** can be used for indefinite periods such as: *at night, at lunchtime*; or for short holiday periods: *at the weekend, at Easter*.
2. Prepositions are almost always omitted before phrases beginning with *last, next, this, that, today, yesterday, tomorrow*:

    Did you attend the lecture *yesterday*?

    I saw that film *last week*.

    I'll bring the photos *next time* I come to your house.

    My parents are going overseas *this year*.

(b) *Prepositions of Place*

These can express:
1. the point itself:

    in, inside—for something contained:

87

There is plenty of food *in* the refrigerator.

You will find some stamps *in* the second drawer of my desk.

My father owns a cottage *in* the country.

Please play *inside*. It's too hot outside.

on, on (to)—the surface:

A coconut tree fell *on to* the roof of his house.

There's a 'Beware of Dogs' sign *on* the gate.

at—a general vicinity:

I'll meet you *at* the Majestic Hotel.

We are still living *at* 64 Primrose Avenue.

Please sit *at* the table when you eat!

I stayed *at* my cousin's house last night.

Turn left *at* the next intersection.

2. away from the point:

   away (from)—general places or vicinities:

   I came *(away) from* the library.

   I stayed *away from* the haunted house.

   He drove *away from* the scene of the accident.

   off—at a distance from the point:

The car ran *off* the road when it knocked the signpost.

The Channel Islands are *off* the coast of France.

The marble rolled *off* the table.

88

across, through, over, along—moving from one place to another:

He kicked the ball *through* the window.
He walked *across* the park to his office.
The boy jumped *over* the fence to get away from the angry bull.
They went *along* the railway line looking for the missing child.

out of—moving from a bounded area:

The gunmen were persuaded to come *out of* the old house.
They chased the dogs *out of* the school compound.

3. towards the point:
   to, into, towards—movement towards a particular place:

I went *to* South America last year.
He went *to* the airport to get his mother.
The car went slowly *into* the tunnel.
The people crowded *into* the streets to watch the National Day celebrations.
The ambulance sped *towards* the entrance of the hospital.

4. towards and then away from the point:
   behind, through, across, round, by, past—movement towards a place and then away from it:

He walked *across* the bridge on his way to the shops.
The car skidded *round* the corner.
They drove *past* the new Town Hall.
The students ran *by* the judges as they crossed the finishing line.

5. vertical and horizontal movement from the point:
up, *down*, *along*, *across*, *over*—movement in relation to a direction:

The old man walked slowly *across* the street.
The dog followed his master *across* the road.
Two schoolboys walked *along* Manchester Street.
She crossed *over* the road to post a letter.
The ball rolled *over* the grass.
The elderly couple climbed slowly *up* the steps.
The boy skated *down* the road on his new skateboard.

6. higher than the point:
over—generally higher than the point:

There is a thick fog *over* the entire city
The planes fly *over* the city to get to the airport.

over—directly above:

The doctor leaned *over* the patient.
He had a deep cut *over* his eye.
A lamp hung *over* the dining-table.

above—directly higher than the point; on a higher level:

We flew *above* the clouds.
There was a dark cloud *above* the bank.

on top of—close to the point; sometimes touching:

The tourists put their bags *on top of* the bus.
You'll find a bottle of ink *on top of* my desk.

7. lower than the point:
   under—directly below:

> The boy hid the money *under* a rock in the garden.
> There is a small stream *under* that bridge.

   underneath—close under; sometimes touching:

> She wore a pretty dress *underneath* her thick coat.

   beneath, *below*—directly under; at a lower level.

> The police found the body *beneath* a pile of wood.

8. neighbouring the point:
   by, *beside*, *next to*—at the side of; near:

> He sat *by* the river reading a book.
> She was standing *by* the window looking at the rain.
> They live in a small village *beside* the sea.
> John likes to sit *beside* his father in the car.
> He sits at the desk *next to* the door.
> I don't like wool *next to* my skin.

   between—relating the positions of one object to more than two objects:

> In the photograph Moira was standing *between* her father and mother.

   among, *amid*—in the middle of (several objects):

> She found her gold chain *amid* the ruins of the burnt house.
> I live *among* the mountains.

91

opposite—facing:

> She sits *opposite* her friend in the school library.

around—surrounding; all round:

> She put a frame *around* the painting. We sat *around* the table and discussed the film.

in front of—at the beginning (in relation to the point):

> He was standing *in front of* a long queue.
> A three-wheeled car was *in front of* my car.

near—close to the point; not far from the point:

> I like to have my bed *near* (to) the window.

5. Conjunctions

The work of a conjunction is to join words, phrases, clauses, or sentences. But while doing so, it can also express certain ideas or notions such as time, contrast, reason, etc.

A. *Types of Conjunctions*

There are two main kinds of conjunctions—**coordinate** and **subordinate**:

(a) *Coordinate Conjunctions*. These join together words, phrases and clauses of equal rank. There are two types of coordinate conjunctions:

1. *Simple Coordinate Conjunctions*: **and, or, but, nor**:

> I looked for the dictionary on the shelf *and* in the cupboard. (phrases)
> The thunder rolled *and* the lightning flashed. (clauses)

92

2. *Correlative Coordinate Conjunctions* (i.e. those that go in pairs): **either . . . or, neither . . . nor, both . . . and, not only . . . but also:**

> Neither tapioca *nor* groundnuts grow well in this soil. (phrases)
> He's *not only* a talented pianist *but also* a good painter. (clauses)

(b) *Subordinate Conjunctions.* These join clauses of unequal rank, i.e. they join subclauses to main clauses:

main clause	subclause
I can buy a car	*when* I have saved a thousand dollars more.

Subordinate conjunctions are of three kinds:

1. *Simple Subordinate Conjunctions:*
   after, (al)though, as, because, before, if, how(ever), like, once, since, that, till, unless, until, when(ever), where(ever), whereas, whereby, whereupon, while, whilst.

2. *Compound Subordinate Conjunctions:*
   (i) except that, for all that, in that, so that, in order that, in order + *to* infinitive, such that.
   (ii) but (that), now (that), providing (that), provided (that), supposing (that), considering (that), given (that), granting (that), granted (that), admitting (that), assuming (that), presuming (that), seeing (that), immediately (that).
   (iii) as far as, as long as, as soon as, in-so-far as, so far as, according to, so as (+ *to* infinitive).
   (iv) as if, as though, in case.
   (v) sooner than, rather than.

3. *Correlative Subordinate Conjunctions* (i.e those that go in pairs):
   if . . . then, (al)though . . . yet/nevertheless, more/less/-*er* . . . that, as . . . as, so . . . as, so . . . (that), such . . . as, such . . . (that), no sooner . . . than, whether . . . or, the . . . the.

Note: Some subordinating conjunctions are also prepositions: as, like, since, until, till, after, before, but.

B. *Functions of Conjunctions*

(a) *Coordination of words*
   (of the same word class):
   Nouns

> The violin *or* the cello is a suitable instrument for her.

Adjectives	The house is beautiful *but* old-fashioned.
Conjunctions	*If* and *when* the electricity is installed, we can move into the house.
Adverbs	He works slowly *but* skilfully.

(b) *Coordination of Clauses*
(or parts of clauses):

Helen plays the guitar *and* she also sings in three languages.
Alex is a bright student *but* he makes little effort.
You may study French *or* you may take Dutch.

Coordination of parts of Clauses: (Note: This occurs where repeated items may be omitted.)

I bought some apples, mangoes *and* (I bought some) limes.

Subjects	*Rashid* and *his sister* are frequent visitors to London.
Verb Phrases	She *writes*, or *used to write*, to her penfriend every month.
Complements	The model is *tall* but *skinny*.
Adverbials	I can mend the hole in your dress *by hand* or *by sewing-machine*.

C. *The Special Meanings of Conjunctions*

The following examples will show that conjunctions are also used to express certain ideas in English:

1. *To express contrast*: (but, yet, nevertheless, still, however)

Adele is intelligent *but* lazy.
We opened the factory a year ago; *still* we are not showing a profit.
Mr Heath is a strict headmaster; *nevertheless* the pupils like him.

94

2. *To express choice (or lack of choice)*: (or, either . . . or, neither . . . nor, else)

> We shall spend our vacation *either* in France *or* in Spain.
> We had to pay a high price *or* (else) he would have sold it to someone else.
> *Either* you will obey the rules *or* you will be sent home.

3. *To express deduction or conclusion*: (for, therefore, so)

> The road was blocked by a landslide, *therefore* we had to take the old road.
> She expected to receive free medical treatment *for* she was a poor widow.
> The business is improving *so* we can give larger bonuses this year.

4. *To express time*: (when, while, as, before, after, till, until, since, whenever)

> My mother has got thinner *since* I last saw her.
> I'll pass on your message *whenever* I see him.
> Mrs Evans wept *after* she received the bad news.

5. *To denote place*: (where, wherever)

> She found her purse *where* she had left it in the bus.
> *Wherever* the cat goes, her kittens follow.

6. *To express manner or comparison*: (as, as . . . as, so . . . as, as if, as though, than)

> He is nearly *as* tall *as* his father.

7. *To express condition*: (if, unless)

> *Unless* the rain stops, the football match will be postponed.
> *If* I win the Welfare Lottery, I'll go for a trip around the world.

8. *To express reason*: (as, because, since)

> The man was sent to prison *because* he had committed a crime.
> *Since* the test is on Friday, you should be reading your books.

9. *To express purpose*: (so that, that, in order that)

> We took a taxi to the stadium *so that* we wouldn't be late for the game.
> A note was sent to all the classrooms *in order that* every boy would know to wear a tie on Mondays.

10. *To express result*: (so . . . that, such . . . that)

> Mr Mooney is *so* busy with his work *that* he has no time for his family.
> There was *such* a crowd at the theatre *that* the police had to be called.

D. *Omission of Conjunctions*

When several items are linked together, the conjunction is usually omitted (or left out) before all items except the last one:

> Please bring me a tomato sandwich, an egg sandwich *and* a bottle of coke.
> This year she is studying History, Geography, French *and* Spanish.

Often the conjunctions are omitted before the adverbs **then, so** and **yet**:

> My income is low (and) *yet* I still manage to live on it.
> Her mother is seriously ill (and) *so* she has to visit the hospital every day.
> The car hit the kerb (and) *then* bounced across the road divider.

6. Interjections

When we wish to express our feelings we sometimes use an **interjection**—a word of exclamation whose only function is to express emotion or feeling.

Interjections can express such emotions as:

surprise:	*Oh*, what a lovely present!
satisfaction:	*Ah*, that's a much neater essay!
great satisfaction:	*Aha*, those are the books I've been looking for.
great surprise:	*Wow*, did you see that goal?
excitement/delight:	*Yipee*, grandfather is coming to visit us!
pain:	*Ouch*, you're treading on my foot!
	Ow, I've hurt myself.
disgust:	*Ugh*, what a filthy kitchen.
pleasure, pain:	*Ooh*, the water's lovely and cool.
	Ooh, my back aches terribly.
exhaustion:	*Phew*, I'm hot!

PART

2

The Mechanics
of English

1 **Punctuation**

Marks of punctuation perform the same function in writing as inflec-
tions, pauses and stresses perform in speech. A question in speech, for
example, has a different rhythm from a command or a statement. Your
voice rises a little for a question, ends on a higher, more intense note
for a command, and falls at the end of a statement.

Your voice relates groups of words or separates them. Without
written marks of punctuation to replace these speech signals, you could
not connect, emphasize, or separate your thoughts in any intelligible
way. These marks help your reader to recognize related units of meaning and ease his task in understanding your ideas. Without these marks
no clear writing is possible. Look at this sentence:

What are we waiting for Robert?

Does the writer mean this? ⟶ What are we waiting for, Robert?
 or this? ⟶ What! Are we waiting for
     Robert?
 or this? ⟶ What are we waiting for?
     Robert.

Unless you use the appropriate punctuation marks, your reader will
always be in doubt.

1. **Using End Marks: The Full Stop (or Period), the Question
Mark, and the Exclamation Mark** . ? !

Read these sentences according to the punctuation at the end:

The Musketeers have won the most applause.
The Musketeers have won the most applause!
The Musketeers have won the most applause?

Under what circumstances might each sentence have been said?

Rules for using Full Stops, Question Marks and Exclamation Marks

Rule 1: Use a full stop to close a declarative sentence (i.e. a sentence which makes a statement).

He is the best waiter at the Majestic Hotel.

Rule 2: Use a full stop to close an imperative sentence (i.e. one which commands, makes a request to which an answer is taken for granted, or entreats).

Eat your rice. (command)
Please stop banging the door. (entreaty)
Will you please come in. (answer taken for granted)

Rule 3: Use a full stop after abbreviations or initials.

approx. (approximately)
advt. (advertisement)
C.O.D. (Cash on delivery)
Asst. Mrs. Dip.Ed.

Rule 4: Use a full stop to indicate a decimal fraction or dollars and cents.

56.7% 10.5 $6.30

Rule 5: Use a question mark to close an interrogative statement (i.e. one which asks a question).

Do you think you did well in the interview?
How are you?

Rule 6: Use an exclamation mark to close an exclamatory sentence (i.e. one which expresses sudden or strong emotion).

Don't touch the wet paint!
Help!
Sit!
How super!

NOTE: Declarative, imperative, or interrogative sentences may become exclamatory if spoken with strong feeling.

She forgot her keys. (declaratory)
She forgot her keys! (exclamatory)
Wait for me. (imperative)
Wait for me! (exclamatory)
Did you see that? (interrogatory)
Did you see that! (exclamatory)

2. Using Apostrophes ⌐'⌐

This is one of the most abused punctuation marks. Have you ever noticed errors like these on shop signs, on menus, in newspapers, on delivery trucks, etc.?

　　†This soup is noted for it's delicious flavour.

　　†We specialize in curtain's and carpet's.

　　†Chinese New Years' Offer!

How could you correct these errors to give the sentences their correct, intended meaning?

†incorrect punctuation

Rules for using Apostrophes

Rule 1: Use the apostrophe to show possession with nouns or indefinite pronouns:

(a) To form the possessive of any singular noun, add an apostrophe and 's' to the noun.	the woman's cat, a man's hobby the girl's sister, Ali's father, Charles's family
(b) To form the possessive of a plural noun ending in 's', add only an apostrophe.	her parents' influence, a boys' school, the Dayaks' houses, a ladies' tailor
(c) To form the possessive of a plural noun that does not end in 's', add an apostrophe and 's'.	children's shoes, policemen's duties, men's clothing
(d) Use the apostrophe to show possession with indefinite pronouns. *Note:* somebody *else's* job	everyone's duty somebody's socks
(e) Use no apostrophe in personal, interrogative, or relative possessives. *Note:* Do not confuse the contractions *it's* and *who's* with the possessives *its* and *whose*.	our, yours, its, hers, theirs, whose It's (It is) mine. The book is in its place. Who's there? Whose boots are these?
(f) Use the apostrophe with expressions of time, space and amount (value).	a three weeks' holiday a day's leave a dollar's worth three months' pay a stone's throw away
(g) In writing the possessive of a compound noun, add an apostrophe plus 's' to the last word of the compound.	mother-in-law's house editor-in-chief's opinion
(h) To show joint ownership, use the apostrophe with the last name only. To show separate ownership, use the apostrophe with each name.	I work at Lee and Son's grocery shop. He got quotations from both Voon's and Tan's companies.

100

Rule 2: Use the apostrophe to make contractions of words or numbers.

o'clock (of the clock)
in the year of '45 (1945)
I'm (I am), I'll (I will)
hadn't (had not), She's (she is)

Rule 3: Use an apostrophe to form the plurals of letters, figures, signs, or words used simply as words.

The number 771318 contains two 7's and two 1's.
There are two M.A.'s, four B.A.'s and nine B.Sc.'s on the staff.

3. Using Quotation Marks ‘ ’

In written material, conversation is identified by the use of quotation marks (or inverted commas)*. They make the page look less monotonous than it might look without them, but their real function is to keep the words of one speaker from becoming confused with those of some other speaker.

The use of quotation marks in themselves is not difficult, but the use of other punctuation marks and capital letters with quotation marks can be confusing.

Rules for using Quotation Marks

Rule 1: Enclose a direct quotation mark:

(a) The direct quotation may be unbroken by explanatory words.

Mr Edwards said, 'My daughter is too young to go steady.'
My mother said to me, 'You are very untidy.'

(b) An extra set of quotation marks must be used if the direct quotation is broken by explanatory words.
Note: The first word of the second part of the broken quotation does not begin with a capital letter unless the word is normally capitalized.

'Help me,' cried the child. 'I cannot get down the ladder.'
'The people of France,' my sister wrote, 'are very friendly.'

(c) Do not put quotation marks around an indirect quotation.

She said, 'I am a film star.'
(direct quotation)
She said that she was a film star.
(indirect quotation)

*This book uses single quotation marks but both single (' ') and double (" ") quotation marks are acceptable in written English.

(d) If the direct quotation consists of two or more sentences unbroken by explanatory material, only one set of quotation marks is necessary.

Mr Lorry quietly held Lucy's hands. 'Don't worry,' he said. 'You know the best and the worst now. You are on your way to see a poor gentleman who has been treated wrongly. If we have a good sea voyage and an easy land journey, you will soon be with him.'

(e) If a quotation has more than one paragraph, use quotation marks at the beginning of each paragraph and at the end of the last paragraph only.

Rule 2: In writing conversation, begin a paragraph for each change of speaker.

'Please show me your driver's license madam,' the policeman said.
'But officer,' Mother protested, 'what was I doing wrong? I wasn't exceeding the speed limit. I didn't go through any red lights.'
'There was only one thing wrong,' he replied. 'You were going the wrong way on a one-way street.'

Rule 3: Enclose in double quotation marks a quotation within a quotation.

'This,' he said, 'is clearly a case of "might is right".'

Rule 4: Use quotation marks (single or double) to draw special attention to a word or words.

The island of Penang is sometimes called 'the Pearl of the Orient'. An 'acronym' is a word which is formed from the initials of a phrase or title.

Rule 5: Use quotation marks to indicate the titles of books, films, plays, songs, stories, works of art, and radio and television programme titles.

Charles Dickens wrote 'Oliver Twist'.
The other day I read Hopkins's poem 'Pied Beauty'.
'Eleanor Rigby' is one of the saddest songs I have ever heard.

Rule 6: Always place quotation marks outside a comma or full stop.

'You have,' she said, 'until Monday to finish the job.'

Rule 7: Always place quotation marks inside a colon or a semi-colon.

She murmured, 'I can't go on'; then she burst into tears.

Rule 8: If a question mark or an exclamation mark belongs with the quotation, place the mark inside the quotation marks; if it belongs to the whole sentence, place it outside.

He kept repeating, 'What shall I do now?'
The children screamed, 'Fire!'
How foolish of Ahmad to say, 'I am never wrong'!
Did Miss Kent say, 'Turn to page sixty'?

4. Using Commas [,]

How do you decide where to use commas? Read these sentences:

I hope you like her Dad because she's my favourite teacher.
Peter the mailman is here.
There is no point in asking honestly.
When are we going to eat Mother.
Ladies and gentlemen lend me your ears.
After beating the egg whites stood in peaks.
Ever since Earl has backed his car into the garage.
Attention mothers day care for babies and children.

Did you have to re-read any of these sentences before the meaning became apparent? You did? That is why commas are necessary to mark pauses and to group words into meaningful patterns. Put commas in the right places to make the meaning clear. Look at the rules on page 104:

"Yes, yes, no, yes, yes, no, no, yes, no, yes, thank you."
© Punch Publications Ltd.

Rules for using Commas

Rule 1: Use a comma or commas to set off a name in direct address.

Mother, may I go out?
May I go out, Mother?
Tell me, Mother, may I go out?

Rule 2: Use commas to separate the parts of a date from one another and from any words following the date.

On Monday, October 29, 1929, the stock market crashed.
The academic year finishes on February 16th, 1980.

Rule 3: Use commas to separate the parts of an address.

Our house in Kuala Kangsar, Perak, was built in June, 1974.
Send entries to:
Jet Set Quiz,
Box 549,
Singapore.

Rule 4: Use a comma after the complimentary close of any letter, and after the salutation.

Dear Farrah,
. . . .
　　　Yours sincerely,

Rule 5: Use commas to separate introductory expressions like *Yes, No, Oh,* and *Well.*

Yes, I can be there by 2 p.m.
Oh, I haven't heard that rumour.
Well, we'll see if we can come.

Rule 6: Use commas to set off expressions that are in apposition.

Joan Thomas, the wife of a well-known politician, is still missing.

Rule 7: Use commas to set off parenthetical material; that is, words or word groups not necessary to the main idea of the sentence.

The rent, by the way, must be paid in advance.
A good salesman, remember, has to know when to keep quiet.

Rule 8: Omit commas if all items in a series are joined by conjunctions.

You have the choice of going to the skating-rink or the swimming-pool or the bowling-alley.

Rule 9: Use commas between two or more adjectives of equal rank when the conjunction is omitted.

The curator of the museum was a helpful, polite, interesting man.

Rule 10: Use a comma to set off words that change a statement into a question or an exclamatory sentence.

You are going, aren't you?
This is fun, isn't it?

Rule 11: Use a comma wherever it will prevent ambiguity; i.e. misreading a sentence.	The day after, George had his appendix removed. With Siti, Aishah hurried to the staff room.
Rule 12: Use a comma (or commas) to set off sharply contrasting expressions.	A liquid, not a powder, should be used. I meant to give money, not labour.
Rule 13: Use a comma (or commas) to set off direct quotations.	'Why,' he said, 'I was only looking in the cupboard for something to eat.'
Rule 14: Use a comma to mark an omission of words.	Lina was wearing a red dress, Lisa a blue one.
Rule 15: Use commas to separate words in a series.	The baby was bald, red, and wrinkled.
Rule 16: Use commas to separate phrases in a series.	Hanna gave Mum a plant, Dad a tie, and me a subscription to 'Her World'.
Rule 17: Use commas to separate clauses in series.	I do not know who he is, how he got in, or why he is here.
Rule 18: Use a comma with the conjunctions *and, but, or, for, yet,* to separate independent clauses.	Mushrooms are good to eat with meat or in soups, but many people do not like them, no matter how they are prepared.
Rule 19: Use a comma after an introductory infinitive or participal phrase, or after an introductory phrase containing a gerund.	After waiting sixteen minutes, I decided to walk. (phrase with gerund) Seeing the trouble I was in, Linda offered me some money. (participal phrase) To prove my point, I produced my birth certificate. (infinitive phrase)
Rule 20: Use a comma to set off sentence modifiers.	Ken leaned back in his chair, touching his forehead thoughtfully, eyes half-closed.

5. Using Semicolons ⎡ ; ⎤

The semicolon is a mark of equality. Stronger than a comma but weaker than a full-stop, it marks a pronounced pause (but not a stop) between two complete statements. The semicolon indicates that these statements are so closely related that they are written as one.

Rules for using Semicolons

Rule 1: Use a semicolon between independent clauses not connected by a conjunction.

The motor spluttered; then it stopped completely.
Farah is quiet and studious; Roslin is noisy and active.

Rule 2: Use a semicolon before such expressions as *however, then, moreover, nevertheless, hence, thus, for instance, consequently, that is,* and *therefore*, if they come between independent clauses not connected by a conjunction.

Our science teacher insists on accuracy; therefore, I prepare my experiments carefully.
You have had three accidents; consequently, you may not borrow the car.

Rule 3: Use a semicolon between items of a series if the items contain internal commas.

Last night at the concert we heard solos by Anna Tombs, first violinist; Melinda Down, soprano; and Edward Woods, baritone.

Rule 4: Use a semicolon to make clear the separation between the main clauses of a compound sentence if the sentence contains other commas.

Marina, I believe, attended the University of Malaya; but her two brothers, I am sure, went to Singapore.

6. Using Colons :

Unlike the semicolon, the colon is not primarily a separating mark. It serves instead as a mark of anticipation to show that something follows: an example, a clarification, a closely related idea.

Rules for using Colons

Rule 1: Use a colon after a statement which introduces examples, usually with such expressions as *the following, these, as follows*.

Malaysia has several large towns: Kuala Lumpur, Ipoh, Penang, Johor Bahru.
My subjects this year are the following: English, Asian History, Malay Studies, and Mandarin.

106

Rule 2: Use a colon between a statement (or quotation) and its clarification.	Robin Hood had a motto: rob the rich and give to the poor. At Gettysburg, Lincoln made his famous speech: 'Fourscore and seven years ago . . . .'
Rule 3: Use a colon between two closely related, balanced items.	Thirty-six cars entered the race: twenty-two finished it.

7. Using Hyphens [-]

Hyphens are used to divide a word at the end of a line or to connect two words which act as one (compound words). As usage of compound words varies from time to time, it is best to consult an up-to-date dictionary. However, the simple rules that follow are useful to remember, especially if you do not have a dictionary at hand.

Rules for using Hyphens

Rule 1: Use a hyphen (or hyphens) in writing certain compound words.	a son-in-law a great-aunt a good-for-nothing a fire-walking ceremony
Rule 2: Use a hyphen in spelling out compound numbers from *twenty-one* to *ninety-nine.*	twenty-three fifty-five eighty-two ninety-six
Rule 3: Use a hyphen in writing out fractions used as adjectives.	The bill was passed by a two-thirds majority.
Rule 4: The suffix *elect* and some prefixes such as *self, vice,* and *ex,* need a hyphen.	president-elect self-esteem self-explanatory vice-president ex-ambassador
Rule 5: Use hyphens between the parts of compound adjectives used before a noun.	ready-to-wear clothing iron-on transfers clean-cut expression two-storey house water-soluble paint loud-talking individual
Rule 6: Use a hyphen in a compound adjective made up of a prefix and a proper noun or adjective.	anti-American non-Malay pre-Roman times

2 Capitalization

English usage requires that sentences begin with capital letters and that proper nouns be capitalized.

Rules for Capitalization

Proper Nouns. Capitalize all proper nouns but capitalize common nouns only when they form part of a proper noun.

Rule 1: Capitalize the names of persons, of the days of the week, and of the months (but *not* the names of the seasons).	Rosli said, 'Last year school opened on the first Monday in January.'
Rule 2: Capitalize the names of religions and religious denominations and other religious terms.	Koran, God, Bible, His teachings, Protestants, Easter, the Month of Ramadan
Rule 3: Capitalize the names of all countries, nationalities, races, and languages. Capitalize all adjectives derived from them.	China—Chinese Sweden—Swedish—Swedes Great Britain—British—English
Rule 4: Capitalize specific geographic and place names.	The Mekong Delta, the Sahara Desert, Bali, Fraser's Hill, Cameron Highlands, Ipoh
Rule 5: Capitalize the names of special organizations, such as schools, businesses, mosques, churches, or political parties.	My father was a student of Malay College. During his lifetime he became a professor at the University of Malaya. He was an active member of the Rotary Club as well as the Umno Political Party. He was also a consultant for the Lee Rubber Company.
Rule 6: Capitalize the names of buildings and other structures; of trains, ships and planes; and of any other special man-made product, including brand or trade names.	Straits Times Building, Suleiman Court, the Thai Embassy, Singapore Airlines, Campbell Road Police Station, Crest, Bubble, Tide

108

Rule 7: Capitalize the names of holidays, of special or important events, of historical periods, and of famous documents. Within such names, do not capitalize prepositions, conjunctions, or the articles *a*, *an*, or *the*.

Chinese New Year, National Day Celebrations, Independence, Christmas Day, Labour Day, the Japanese Occupation

General Rules + Other Nouns

Rule 8: Capitalize the first word of every sentence.

Rule 9: A poet may capitalize the first word of each line of poetry if he wishes (including rhymes and limericks).

Apartment House
A filing-cabinet of human lives
Where people swarm like bees in
tunnelled hives,
Each to his own cell in the
towered comb,
Identical and cramped—we call it
home.

Rule 10: Capitalize the first word of a direct quotation.

Confucius wrote: 'Not to alter one's faults is to be faulty indeed'.

Rule 11: Capitalize the titles of literary, musical and art works. In such titles, capitalize prepositions, conjunctions and the articles (*a, an, the*) only if they precede the title.

*My favourite poem is Carl Sandburg's *Lost*; my favourite novel is Paul Gallico's *Matilda*; and my favourite painting is William Dobell's *The Billy Boy*.

Rule 12: Capitalize titles of persons, including degrees, and their abbreviations when used as part of a proper noun.
Note: Do *not* capitalize a title not used as part of a proper noun.

John D. Rockefeller, Jr., founded Rockefeller Centre.

Mr Stevens, our mayor, spoke at the dinner.

Rule 13: Capitalize the names of school language subjects but *not* of general subjects. Capitalize the names of these general subjects only if they refer to a specific course.

In his first year of university he took three subjects: Biology, Chemistry and Physics. He also had to take a foreign language.

*Use quotation marks around titles in hand-written English (see *Rule 5*, page 102).

109

Rule 14: Capitalize the official names of government departments, the titles of high-ranking officials that precede or follow a name or that stand alone, and names of legislative bills and acts.

the *A*mbassador, the *S*ecretary of *S*tate, the *P*rime *M*inister, *P*resident Tito, the *D*epartment of *I*nland *R*evenue, the *T*reaty of *V*ersailles

General

Rule 15: Capitalize the pronoun *I* and its contractions.

I, *I*'m, *I*'ll, *I*'d, *I*'ve

Rule 16: Capitalize the names of objects, animals, seasons and ideas, when treated as if they were human.

'Sport, that wrinkled *C*are derides, And *L*aughter holding both his sides'—Milton.

Rule 17: Capitalize *north, south, east* and *west* and their derivatives (e.g. northern, southwest) when they refer to sections of a country or the world. Do not capitalize these words to indicate direction only.

President Snow is going on a tour of the *F*ar *E*ast.
Turn *east* at the next corner.

Rule 18: Capitalize the first word and all nouns in the salutation of a letter, as well as the first word of the complimentary close.

Dear *U*ncle *T*ony, . . .
*M*y dear *B*etty, . . .
*Y*ours sincerely/faithfully/truly . . .

Rule 19: Capitalize family relationship terms only when they are used with a name or when they take the place of a name. Capitalize nicknames and other words used as names.

His *A*unt *E*nid gave him the skateboard.
My *m*other envies my *a*unt because of her exciting life as a model.

Rule 20: Capitalize A.M. and P.M. (though this rule is not rigid). Capitalize initials and abbreviations of words that themselves would be capitalized if written in full.

P.T.A. (Parents'-Teachers' Association)
Letterite *C*o. *L*td. (Company Limited)
*C*apt. Ashad.

3 Improving Spelling

Poor spelling is an individual matter frequently related to faulty sight, hearing and memory. Unfortunately, not only does incorrect spelling interfere with communication, but it also misrepresents you. However, anyone can learn to spell if he wants to by just attacking words from four directions: seeing, hearing, speaking, and writing.

"We'll be sorry to see you go, Miss Witherspoon—your unique spelling has given us many hilarious moments."

© Cartoon Features Syndicate

Ways of Learning to Spell

A. *Look at words carefully*

1. Circle or underline words that contain trouble spots for you; then concentrate on those letters or letter combinations:

   w<u>o</u>men   fri<u>e</u>nd   troub<u>le</u>
   defin<u>ite</u>   f<u>o</u>rty   de<u>s</u>cribe

2. Use mental pictures. Study the features of the word: the tall letters, the ones that drop below the line, their position in a word. Stare at the shape of a word. Try to visualize the contours of a word.

3. Pair a troublesome word with one that you know how to spell:

   before   more   quiet   diet

4. Find other words within a word. A nonsense sentence might help:

> At a *villa* in Spain lived a *villain*.
> *Fry* your *friend* and that's the *end*.
> A soft drink is *pleasant* for an *ant*.
> It takes a *real* man to *realize* his faults.

5. Use jingles or memory reminders, or any other type of association:

-ar	This particul*ar* popul*ar* st*ar* used to be a burgl*ar* with a sc*ar*.
-ense	He grew t*ense* when they said the exp*ense* for def*ense* didn't make s*ense*.
-ance	He wants an adv*ance* in his allow*ance*.
for*ty*	for*ty* for*ts*
se*parate*	My *pa* hit a *rat* while playing golf.
gl*imp*se	Put an *imp* in gl*imp*se.
twe*lf*th	Put an *elf* in twe*lf*th.
pri*son*	There's a *son* in pri*son*.
holiday	Holiday means holy day. Both have one *l*.
all right	All are right.
grammar	3 pairs: 2 r's; 2 a's; 2 m's.
embarrass	3 pairs: 2 a's; 2 r's; 2 s's.

B. *Learn to hear and to say words correctly*
1. Notice the sounds that make words. Make sure you pronounce words correctly yourself. The following are some words that are misspelled chiefly because of mispronunciation:

(i) omitting the sound of a letter:

escape	height	perhaps (not praps)
modern	exactly	performance
across	literature	

(ii) inserting an extra letter:

athlete (not ath-a-lete)	entrance (not en-ter-ance)
hungry (not hung-er-ry)	lightning (not light-en-ing)

(iii) transposing letters:

perspiration (not prespiration)
introduce (not in-ter-duce)
library (not lib-ra-rary)

112

2. Pay attention to words with silent letters. When writing it is advisable to actually pronounce the silent letter:

listen	=	lis *t*en
handsome	=	han*d* some
cupboard	=	cu*p* board
mortgage	=	mor*t* gage

3. Pay attention to words with tricky vowels because their pronunciation does not provide foolproof clues to their spelling. Exaggerate the pronunciation to yourself as you write such words:

ben E fit	con FI dent	tem PO rary
med I cine	cit I zen	mag A zine

C. *Study and apply rules*

Thousands of words in English are spelled according to fixed rules. Below are some of these rules:

Rules for Spelling

Rule 1: Applying Prefixes (see page 198 on Derivations). When applying prefixes, do not drop any letters, (or add any), either from the root word or the prefix.

dis + satisfied = dissatisfied
un + equal = unequal
mis + spell = misspell
im + mortal = immortal

Rule 2: Do not confuse words that end in *-cede, -ceed,* or *-sede.*

cede: ac*cede*, con*cede*, inter*cede*, pre*cede*, re*cede*
ceed: ex*ceed*, pro*ceed*, suc*ceed*
sede: super*sede*

Rule 3: Internal spelling: words containing *ie* or *ei:*

(a) When the sound is long *e*, write *ie* except after *c*.

re*cei*pt, *cei*ling, de*cei*ve

(b) If a *c* does not come before a long *e* sound, words are spelled *ie*.

bel*ie*ve, n*ie*ce, f*ie*rce, th*ie*f, f*ie*ld, pr*ie*st

(c) If the words do not have a long *e* sound they are spelt *ei* (pronounced *a*).

fr*ei*ght, w*ei*ght

113

> Use *i* before *e* except after *c*,
> Or when sounded as *a*
> As in *neighbour* and *weigh*;
> But *their*, *weird* and *either*,
> *Foreign*, *seize*, *neither*,
> *Leisure*, *forfeit* and *height*,
> Are exceptions spelled right.

Rule 4: In English *q* is always followed by *u*.

*qu*arrel	*qu*aint
*qu*antity	*qu*arantine

Rule 5: In English the letters *ph* are sounded like *f*.

geogra*ph*y	em*ph*asize
*ph*otography	*ph*ysician
tele*ph*one	so*ph*isticated
apostro*ph*e	*ph*enomenon
*ph*rase	*ph*os*ph*ate
catastro*ph*e	

Adding Suffixes

Rule 6: To add a letter or a suffix to a word that ends in *y* do the following:

(a) If the vowel precedes the *y*, merely add the letter or the suffix without change.

bu*y*, buy*s*, buy*ing*
emplo*y*, emplo*yment*
enjo*y*, enjo*yable*

(b) If a consonant preceeds the *y*, change the *y* to *i* unless the suffix is *-ing*.

cr*y*, cr*ying*, cr*ied*
funn*y*, funn*ier*, funn*iest*
marr*y*, marr*ied*, marr*iage*
laz*y*, laz*iness*

Rule 7: If a word ends in *ie*, change those letters to *y* when adding the suffix *-ing*.

unt*ie*, unt*ying*
l*ie*, l*ying*
d*ie*, d*ying*

Rule 8: When adding a prefix beginning with a vowel, double a final consonant following a single vowel if:

(a) the word contains only one syllable;

swim + *ing* = swim*ming*
run + *er* = run*ner*
rob + *ery* = rob*bery*
drop + *ed* = drop*ped*, etc.

114

(b) the word contains more
than one syllable and is
accented on the last
syllable.

begin$'$ + *ing* = begin*ning*
prefer$'$ + *ed* = prefer*red*
occur$'$ + *ence* = occur*rence*
regret$'$ + *able* = regret*table*

Rule 9: When adding a suffix,
do not double the final consonant
if:

(a) the suffix begins with a
consonant;

defe*r*, defe*r*ment
gla*d*, gla*dly*

(b) the accent does not fall
on the last syllable;

or$'$de*r*, orde*red*   o$'$pen, ope*ning*
hap$'$pe*n*, happe*ned*
of$'$fe*r*, offe*ring*

(c) more than one vowel
precedes the final con-
sonant, or two consonants
follow a vowel.

disappea*r*, disappea*rance*
hu*rt*, hu*rting*
ame*nd*, ame*ndment*

Rule 10: (Words ending in silent
e):

(a) If a suffix beginning with
a vowel is added to a word
that ends in silent *e* preceded by a consonant, drop
the final *e*.

los$\cancel{e}$ + *ing* = losing
ador$\cancel{e}$ + *able* = adorable
hop$\cancel{e}$ + *ed* = hoped
matur$\cancel{e}$ + *ity* = maturity

(b) If the silent *e* is preceded by
a vowel, the final *e* is
frequently dropped.
(Exceptions: dyeing, hoeing,
ageing.)

continu$\cancel{e}$, continu*ing*, continu*ous*,
continu*ation*.
argu$\cancel{e}$, argu*ing*

(c) If a suffix begins with a consonant, keep the final *e*.
(Exceptions: truly, wholly,
duly, awful, argument.)

us*e* + *f*ul = useful
hom*e* + *l*ess = homeless
nin*e* + *t*y = ninety
puzzl*e* + *m*ent = puzzlement
sincer*e* + *l*y = sincerely

Exceptions to Rule 10:

(a) If words are compounded,
keep the final *e*.

on*e* + self = oneself

115

(b) If the final *e* is preceded by *c* or *g*, retain the final *e* before a suffix beginning with *a* or *o* (*able*, *ouse*).

notice + *a*ble = notic*ea*ble

(c) If the word ends in double *e* (ee), drop an *e* only before a syllable beginning with *e*, e.g. *ed, en*.

agr*ee* + *ed* = agr*ee*d
disagr*ee* + *ed* = disagr*ee*d

Rule 11: If a word ends in *c*, add a *k* before a suffix beginning with *e*, *i*, or *y*.

picni*c*, picni*ck*ing
pani*c*, pani*ck*y, pani*ck*ed
traffi*c*, traffi*ck*ing, traffi*ck*er
mimi*c*, mimi*ck*ed, mimi*ck*ing

Rule 12: (Words ending in *-ly*, *-el* and *-ll*):

(a) Words ending in *-el* generally double the *l* even though the accent does not fall on the last syllable.

trav*el*, trav*ell*er
quarr*el*, quarr*ell*ed
jew*el*, jew*ell*er

(b) *Full* drops an *l* when it is at the end of a word.

power*ful*, play*ful*,
delight*ful*, wonder*ful*

(c) Generally words ending in *-ll* drop an *l* when they are part of another word. (Exceptions: full—fullness; fill, refill.)

ski*ll* − ski*l*ful
wi*ll* − wi*l*ful
fu*ll* − fu*l*fil

(d) Words ending in *-ly* do not drop the preceding *l*.

faithful + *ly* = faithfu*lly*
also: dreadful, natural, general, usual, local, equal

Rule 13: Forming Plurals of Nouns (see page 16).

D. *Take an interest in words*

Take words apart to find their meanings. Study prefixes, suffixes, and root words (see pages 198-202 on Derivations).

E. *Learn to spell words that sound alike (Homonyms)*

In the gold-rush days of America, people often thought they had 'struck it rich', when actually they had just found a worthless mineral called 'fool's gold'. Fool's gold and real gold are really two quite different things but because they look so alike, people often mix them up.

The same sort of confusion is likely to occur when we come across words known as **homonyms**—words that sound alike but differ in meaning and usually in spelling. That is why it is important to know the meaning of a word in order to be able to spell it.

Can you distinguish the meanings between these pairs (or groups) of words?

ail	bell	cent	cite
ale	belle	scent	sight
		sent	site
air	berth		
heir	birth	ceiling	clause
		sealing	claws
aisle	berry		
I'll	bury	cell	chord
isle		sell	cord
	blew		
allowed	blue	cellar	core
aloud		seller	corp
	boar		
altar	bore	cereal	council
alter		serial	counsel
	board		
ascent	bored	cheap	crews
assent		cheep	cruise
	bolder		
bail	boulder	check	currant
bale		cheque	current
	bough		
ball	bow		
bawl			
	boy		
bare	buoy		
bear			
	brake		
baron	break		
barren			
	bread		
base	bred		
bass			
	buy		
be	by		
bee			
	canvas		
beach	canvass		
beech			
	coarse		
bean	course		
been			
	cede		
beat	seed		
beet			

"I said diet, not dye it." © Colin Earl

117

cymbal	foul	hour	main
symbol	fowl	our	mane
days	frees	idle	manner
daze	freeze	idol	manor
dear	gage	idyll	mare
deer	gauge	in	mayor
dew	gait	inn	marshal
due	gate	incite	martial
descent	gamble	insight	meat
dissent	gambol	its	meet
die -d/-ing	gilt	it's	medal
dye -d/-ing	guilt	key	meddle
doe	grate	quay	metal
dough	great	knew	mettle
draft	groan	new	miner
draught	grown	knight	minor
earn	guessed	night	missed
urn	guest	knot	mist
ewe	hail	not	moan
you	hale	know	mown
faint	hair	no	morning
feint	hare	knows	mourning
fair	hall	nose	muscle
fare	haul	lead(n)	mussel
feat	heal	led	none
feet	heel	leak	nun
	he'll	leek	
find	hear	lessen	oar
fined	here	lesson	ore
firs	heard	licence	one
furs	herd	license	won
flea		lightening	pail
flee	higher	lightning	pale
flew	hire	loan	pain
flue	him	lone	pane
flour	hymn	loot	pair
flower	hoard	lute	pare
for	horde	made	pear
fore	hoarse	maid	passed
four	horse	mail	past
forth	hole	male	patience
fourth	whole		patients

118

pause	wright	stair	waist
paws	write	stare	waste
peace	ring	stake	wait
piece	wring	steak	weight
peal	road	stationary	ware
peel	rode	stationery	wear
pedal	rowed	steal	where
peddle	roam	steel	way
peer	Rome	stile	weigh
pier	role	style	weak
plain	roll	straight	week
plane	root	strait	weather
plum	route	suite	whether
plumb	rose	sweet	which
pores	rows	tail	witch
pours	sail	tale	whirled
practice	sale	tears	world
practise	sauce	tiers	who's
praise	source	their	whose
prays	scene	there	wood
preys	seen	they're	would
presence	sea	threw	yolk
presents	see	through	yoke
principal	seam	throne	
principle	seem	thrown	
profit	sew	tide	
prophet	so	tied	
rains	sow	to	
reigns	sighs	too	
reins	size	two	
raise	sight	told	
rays	site	tolled	
raze	soar	trait	
rap	sore	tray	
wrap	soared	troop	
read	sword	troupe	
reed	sole	vain	
real	soul	vein	
reel	son	vale	
right	sun	veil	
rite			

119

F. *Learn to Spell Words that are Similar in Appearance*

The following pairs of words are often wrongly used for each other. They are not homonyms, but are words that are confused partly because of mispronunciation and partly because of their similarity of spelling.

Word	Meaning
accept (vb)	to receive
except	not including; other than
addition	something added
edition	one printing of a book, newspaper, magazine, etc.
advice (n)	verbal help given to another
advise (vb)	to tell someone what one thinks should be done
affect (vb)	to cause some change; to influence
effect (vb)	to cause, produce
(n)	a result
alternate (vb)	to follow by turns
alternative (adj)	the choice between two things that may be done, had, etc.
beside (prep)	next to; close to the side of
besides (prep)	in addition to; as well as
breath (n)	air taken in and out of the lungs
breathe (vb)	to take air into (and let out of) the lungs
childish (adj)	typical of a child (e.g. someone's actions unsuitable for an adult)
childlike (adj)	of or typical of a child (but considered natural)
choose (vb)	to pick out or select from a number of items
chose	past tense of 'choose'
clothes	garments, e.g. dresses, shirts, worn on the body
cloths	pieces of fabric or material, usually used for cleaning purposes
complement (vb)	to make something complete
(n)	the number or quantity needed to make something complete
compliment (vb)	to praise someone
(n)	an expression of praise, admiration, or respect
credible (adj)	trustworthy; deserving to be believed
creditable (adj)	deserving praise, honour, approval, etc.
dairy	a place where milk, butter and cheese are kept or made or sold
diary	a book containing a daily record of events in a person's life

120

Word	Meaning
decease (n)	death
disease (n)	an illness caused by an infection, etc. and not by an accident
defer (vb)	to delay; to put off until another time
differ (vb)	to be unlike; to disagree
dependant (n)	a person who depends on another for material support (food, clothing, money, etc.)
dependent (adj)	being influenced, controlled, or supported by another person or thing
desert (vb)	to leave completely; to leave empty
dessert (n)	sweet food served at the end of a meal
emigrate (vb)	to leave one's own country in order to go and live in another
immigrate (vb)	to come into a country in order to settle there
eligible (adj)	suitable to be chosen
illegible (adj)	(writing, etc.) that cannot be read
elder (n)	the older of two people
older (adj)	the comparative form of the adjective 'old' (i.e. it is followed by 'than')
eminent (adj)	famous; admired
imminent (adj)	something that is going to happen very soon
every day (adv)	once in each day
everyday (adj)	common, ordinary, usual
formally	in a dignified manner
formerly	in earlier times
human (n)	related to mankind
humane (adj)	showing human kindness
later	happening after the expected time
latter (adj)	nearer to the end; coming after
loose (adj)	not fastened or tied up; free
lose (vb)	1. fail to keep something; 2. to be defeated
memorable (adj)	something that is worth remembering; something special
memorial (n)	an object (e.g. a monument) in a public place in memory of a person, event, etc.
moral (adj)	concerning good behaviour, character, actions, etc.
morale (n)	the moral condition or state of mind of a person or group of people
recede (vb)	to go before
roceed (vb)	to continue; to start

121

Word	Meaning
precedent	a former action that may serve as a guide to present actions
president	a head of a government or other institution
price	an amount of money for which a thing is offered, sold or bought
prize	a reward given to someone who is successful in studies, games, competitions, etc.
quiet (adj)	at rest; the opposite of noisy
quite (adv)	completely, perfectly, entirely
raise (vb)	to lift up; to increase something
rise (vb)	to get up; to go up
respectfully	in a polite, courteous manner
respectively	each separately in the order mentioned
than	a conjunction used in comparisons, e.g. older than
then	adverb of time
vacation	a holiday; a holiday period when schools, etc. are closed
vocation	a job for which one is particularly suited

PART

Expression in English

The English language is rich in vocabulary, including its ways of expressing distinctions of meaning. It is particularly rich in idiomatic expressions. What then is an idiom? An idiom is a number of words which, taken together, mean something different from the meanings of the words when they stand alone.

Idiomatic expressions can be found in the daily speech of native speakers of English, on the radio, in novels, newspaper and magazine articles, rather than in formal writing. Idioms can be short or long but, as a general rule, they cannot be changed (i.e. the words making up the idiom always remain in the same position).

It is the idiomatic part of English (or of any language) that is most difficult for a foreign student to master. Thus, he needs to note the exact words that make up any idiom and also the exact arrangement of those words, besides learning the special meanings of idioms.

1   Idiomatic Adjective and Noun Phrases

1. Phrases composed of an Adjective and a Noun
an absent-minded person a forgetful, inattentive person
advanced in years/life growing old; elderly
— **apple-pie order** in perfect order
— **an armchair critic** a person who critically judges others' work and gives
    advice, but who has not himself experienced doing the work
— **backstairs influence** secret and usually unfair influence
— **bad blood** unfriendliness or bad feelings between two people
— **a bad egg, a bad penny** a bad character

bad language swear words

a big shot an important person, usually someone wealthy and influential

— **a blind date** a social meeting of two people (usually a boy and girl) who have not met before *Rendezvous mit einer Unbekannten*

a born teacher one who has a natural talent for teaching

a bosom friend a very close, trusted friend

broad daylight the full light of day; very bright and clear

— **broken English** imperfect, ungrammatical English

a burning question a matter having to be dealt with at once; an urgent, important matter

a chicken-hearted person a timid, cowardly person

— **a close-fisted person** a miser; someone who is stingy

— **a close shave** a narrow escape from danger, an accident, etc.

— **a cock-and-bull story** an invented story, one hard to believe

a cold war a serious political struggle between countries which does not actually result in fighting

— **a confirmed bachelor** a man who has no desire to marry; usually a man firmly settled in his way of life *eingefleischter Junggeselle*

— **a country cousin** a person who is simple and inexperienced and not used to city life

crocodile tears insincere tears; pretended sorrow

— **a dark horse** a person who competes successfully against another although little is known about him

— **a dead-end job** a job without prospects; a job that leads to nothing further *Job ohne Aufstiegsmöglichkeiten*

a dog-eared book a book where the corners of the pages have been turned down with use

— **donkey's years** a very long time

a double agent a person who works secretly for two opposing sides without either of the sides knowing

— **double Dutch** speech or writing that one cannot understand *Kauderwelsch*

— **Dutch courage** courage brought about by drinking alcohol

— **a Dutch treat** entertainment (a meal, a film, etc.) at which each person pays his own bill

— **an easy mark/victim** somebody who can easily be cheated or treated badly

elbow room space in which to move and act freely

a fair copy a neat, legible copy

a false alarm a warning of something bad, which does not happen

a fast colour a colour which does not run out of the material when washed or dried

fast living a person who spends too much money in enjoying life

a fishy story an unlikely story; an untrue tale

— **a flying visit** a very short visit *stehe*

— **a foregone conclusion** a result that is certain, sure *von vornherein fest-*

— **forty winks** a short nap or sleep *Nickerchen*

French leave absence from work that is taken without permission

the generation gap the difficulties arising when younger and older people do not understand each other's way of life *Generationsproblem ~ konflik*

a going concern a successful, thriving business

a golden opportunity a very good opportunity

a good Samaritan a person who helps a stranger in difficulties

— **a grass widow** a wife who is alone because her husband is away temporarily *Strohwitwe*

half-hearted having no enthusiasm for a particular task

— **the happy medium** the middle course of doing something when opposite ways are suggested

hard cash actual money, not a cheque, etc.

a hard drinker a person who drinks large quantities of alcohol

hard drugs the strongest drugs, which lead to <u>addiction</u>, e.g. heroin

— **a hard and fast rule** a rule that cannot be changed; fixed, unchangeable rules *bindende*

hard labour hard, manual work usually done as a punishment *Pantoffelhe*

— **a henpecked husband** one who is dominated and nagged at by his wife

high time at the most important point of time

a hot line a direct telephone line between heads of governments, to be used at times of great difficulty *heißer Draht*

hot news very recent, important or sensational news

— **hot water** trouble

— **hush money** a bribe paid to keep a matter secret from the public *Schweigege*

— **a hushed-up affair** an affair or matter that is kept secret by forcing silence about it

— **idle gossip/talk** gossip; talk that is wasteful and useless

— **an inside job** a theft committed by someone 'inside' a building, i.e. by an employee, not a stranger *von Insidern begangen*

an iron will a very strong will

— **a jail bird** a man who has spent a lot of time in prison *Knastbruder*

a knowing look a look which suggests that the person is well-informed of a matter

a ladies' man a man who likes to be with women or who likes to please them

— **a last fling** the last opportunity for pleasure or amusement before having to stop

126

the last straw an additional problem which makes the present problem(s) or trouble(s) even more difficult and unbearable

a laughing stock a person who is unkindly laughed at by everyone

left-wing party a political group favouring great political change

a light-fingered person a person who is in the habit of stealing small things

a light sleeper a person easily awakened from sleep

a long term (plan) for or in the distant future

a maiden name (for Christians) the surname (or father's name) a woman bore before she got married

a marked man one who is regarded with suspicion because of some earlier scandal

monkey business/tricks behaviour which causes trouble; behaviour which is full of tricks

the naked eye the eye unaided by any instrument, e.g. binoculars

a narrow escape an escape which nearly failed

an odd-job man a man who does various types of work (usually manual) for pay

the odd man out a person who does not fit in with others because he does not share their interests, etc.; someone who does not mix easily with others

old hat out-of-date, no longer fashionable

an old maid an unmarried lady who is no longer young

an old wives' tale an ancient idea or belief handed down by tradition; usually foolish, unscientific beliefs

one-track mind a (person's) mind that is limited and thinks of only one thing at a time

an open-door policy the idea of permitting traders from all countries to trade freely in a particular country

an open secret something supposed to be a secret but which in fact is known to everyone

a package deal an offer or agreement which includes a number of things all of which must be taken

a package tour a completely planned holiday at a fixed price arranged by a company

a passing fancy a temporary liking for something or someone

a pep talk a friendly talk to give encouragement to win (a game) or to complete something well

a pet aversion something or someone greatly disliked

pin money a wife's allowance for her personal needs

plain dealing truthfulness and honesty (especially in business)

plain sailing a plan or action that is simple and free from trouble

a practical joke a trick played on a person to make him look silly and to give amusement to others

a ramshackle house/car falling to pieces; badly in need of repair

(in) a rash moment doing something hastily without thinking of the results

a raw deal unjust or cruel treatment

a ready-made dress a dress bought in a shop; not made specially for the buyer

ready money money which is immediately available in coins or notes

right-wing members of a political party favouring fewer political changes

a rolling stone a person who travels around a lot without staying in any one place or job for long

a rough guess an approximate calculation or estimate

a rude awakening/shock a sudden and violent shock

sales talk talking intended to persuade or sell, by praising what is for sale

second best next to the best; second in value or importance

second nature some acquired habit or skill which seems perfectly natural to someone; a very firmly fixed habit

second rate of inferior quality

second sight an ability to foresee future events

second thoughts a change of mind, attitude or decision after thinking about the matter

a security risk a person who is a risk to a country's security because of his political activities; one whose loyalty is doubted

a shady character a person of very doubtful honesty or character

short change less money than the correct change one should receive

a short cut an easier method of doing something or getting somewhere; a quicker more direct way

sick leave leave given because of illness

a side-line work one does apart from one's regular job

a sleeping partner a business partner who provides a share of the capital for a venture but does not take an active part in its operation

small change money in coins of small value

the small hours the early morning hours just after midnight

small talk trivial, light conversation on unimportant topics

a small-time business a business limited in activity and profits; unimportant

a smart aleck a person who annoys others by claiming to know everything

a soft spot a feeling of special fondness for something or someone

a sore point a matter which irritates or hurts when it is mentioned

spare time leisure time; free time

a spending spree an outing during which one spends a lot of money

a splitting headache a very severe and painful headache

a spring clean a thorough cleaning (usually of a house)

a square deal a fair bargain or fair treatment

a square meal a meal with adequate food; a satisfying meal

a stag party a party where only men are allowed to be present

a stand-up fight a hard fight, fought either with words or with fists

strong language angry language consisting of many swear words; curses

a sugar daddy an older man who has a relationship, especially sexual, with a younger woman, providing her with money and presents

a sweeping statement a generalization; a statement not careful or correct in its details

a sweet tooth (of a person) with a liking for things that are sweet and sugary

take-home pay/wages the amount a person receives after taxes have been deducted

a tall order a request which is unreasonably difficult to grant or carry out

tall talk boastful talk

teething troubles troubles and difficulties which occur during the early stages of an activity or enterprise, but which will lessen with time

a thick-skinned person a person who is not easily offended; insensitive

a third party another person in addition to the two in question

a tight spot/corner a difficult situation

a tight squeeze to be very crowded (as in a vehicle containing too many people)

top brass officers of high rank in the armed forces

top people people in the highest positions in their professions

tough luck bad luck; hard luck

a trend-setter a person who starts a new fashion which becomes popular

(the) upper crust the higher classes of society

(the) upper hand control

a vicious circle a problem which is difficult to solve because the cause and the result of the problem are interdependent

a wet blanket a person who discourages others or prevents them from enjoying what they are doing

a wild goose chase a search for something which has no chance of being successful

a willing horse a helpful person, who often gets all the work to do

a working knowledge enough practical knowledge to do something

a working lunch/dinner a meal at which the people who attend discuss business

2. Idiomatic Noun Phrases (consisting of two nouns)

a bear hug a rough, tight hug

the bottom of the ladder in the least important position

(the) brain drain the movement of skilled/professional people from countries where they were trained to other countries where they can earn more money

a brain wave a clever idea; sudden inspiration

a clean bill of health a certificate or announcement that someone is healthy

birds of a feather people of the same kind (often bad) who like each other's company

a bone of contention something that causes argument

castles in the air plans which cannot be carried out or which will probably not succeed

a feather in one's cap a deserved honour that one is proud of

a fish out of water a person who feels uncomfortable because he is in a strange place/or among people who are very different from himself

by fits and starts at irregular intervals; not continuously; starting and stopping

the gift of the gab a person fluent in speech; a persuasive speaker

by hook or by crook by any means possible

a jack of all trades a person who can do many different kinds of work but who may not be good at any of them

the long arm of the law the police

the life and soul (of the party) the person who is the centre of attraction because he is amusing and lively

the lion's share the greater part; an unfairly large share

a man about town a man who is used to living in the city and associating with well-known, fashionable people

a man of iron a cruel, hard person

the man in the street the ordinary, average man

a man of means a rich man

a pack of lies a whole lot of untruths

the rank and file the masses; ordinary people without special positions

the root of all evil the origin or cause of evil, usually money

a shot in the arm something which acts to bring back a happy state or condition

130

a shot in the dark a guess which is not supported by arguments; a wild guess

a slap in the face an action that seems to be aimed at someone else; a rebuff

a slip of the tongue something said unintentionally (and is usually regretted)

a snake in the grass a cunning, harmful person who pretends to be a friend; a false friend

a stone's throw a short distance; the distance one would cover in throwing a stone

a storm in a teacup a big fuss made over a small, trivial event

the talk of the town a person or event that is causing great excitement and is the subject of much discussion

the tricks of the trade the best and most successful ways of doing good business

the ups and downs (of something) the good and bad times, the happy and sad times

the writing on the wall an indication that something bad or difficult is about to happen

3. Pairs of Adjectives

Many idiomatic phrases are formed by two adjectives joined together by **and**, **but**, or **or**. The order of such adjective pairs is fixed and needs to be memorized.

for better (or) for worse whatever happens; even if there are difficulties

(to be) cut and dried fixed or settled; unlikely to be changed

(by) fair means or foul somehow; in any way, good or bad

fair and square in a fair, reasonable way; honestly; justly

(to be) few and far between infrequent; rare; not happening too often

(to be) free and easy cheerful and unworried; casual

(to be left) high and dry left without support; without help

high and low everywhere

(to act) high and mighty too proud

(to blow) hot and cold to be changeable in one's opinions

the long and (the) short of it the general state of affairs; all that needs to be said about something

more or less almost; nearly

more and more increasingly; becoming larger

rough and ready simple; without comfort; not exact

short and sweet not wasting time (or words); direct; brisk

(through) thick and thin through both good and bad times

131

Others which need no explanation:

ancient and modern	past and present
dead and gone/dead and	rich and poor
buried	right and wrong
good, bad or indifferent	safe and sound
great and small	slow but sure
meek and mild	spick and span
null and void	

4. Pairs of Nouns

In English there are a number of pairs of nouns which always go together to form an idiom. In these pairs, too, the order of the words is fixed.

arts and sciences	ladies and gentlemen	rack or ruin
bag and baggage	land and sea	rain or shine
bow and arrow	life and limb	rhyme or reason
bread and butter	light and shade	skin and bone
bucket and spade	lock and key	son and heir
flesh and blood	for love or money	stocks and shares
friend or foe	male and female	stuff and nonsense
hammer and tongs	man and beast	sun, moon or stars
hand and foot	men and women	tea or coffee
head over heels	mother and child	tooth and nail
heart and soul	odds and ends	town and country
heaven and earth	part and parcel	use and abuse
horse and cart	pen and ink/paper	vice and virtue
house and home	pins and needles	wear and tear
hue and cry	pipe and tobacco	wife and children
judge and jury	profit and loss	wind and weather
king and queen	pros and cons	

5. Compound Adjectives

Adjectives made up of a few words are often found in newspaper reports and in colloquial English. Such adjectives are always joined by hyphens. Look at the examples below:

bumper-to-bumper traffic cars that are very close together one after another

a **hand-me-down dress** a dress used by someone after belonging to another

a **happy-go-lucky person** a careless person; someone who does not think or plan carefully

a hit-and-run driver a driver who drives away after an accident without stopping to find out about damage or injuries

a much-talked-of affair something which is the subject of much discussion

a nine-to-five job a job in which the working hours are from nine in the morning to five in the evening

an open-and-shut case a case (e.g. a murder) which is easy to settle or solve

an out-of-the-way place a place that is distant and far away from people and places

ready-to-wear clothes clothes not especially made for the buyer; clothes bought in a shop

a round-the-clock service a twenty-four hour service, e.g. a petrol station open all day and all night

a run-of-the-mill job an ordinary, unexciting job; not special

a smash-and-grab robbery a robbery done quickly, usually by breaking windows or showcases, taking away valuables and running away

a stay-at-home person a person in the habit of staying at home and not liking to travel

a well-to-do man/woman a rich person

2 Idiomatic Commonplace Comparisons (Similes)

In conversation, English-speaking people often use striking comparisons to give flavour to their speech. Such expressions—or similes—make comparisons in the imagination between two things. These two items of comparison are usually connected by the words **as** or **like**.

Similes can be based on the qualities of persons, other living creatures, or objects. Although there are many hundreds of similes in the English language—and it is not difficult to think of new ones—only the better-known ones are listed below.

1. Similes based on the Distinctive Qualities of Persons

as bashful/shy as a schoolgirl
as devoted as a mother
as frisky as a two-year old
as happy as a child/king/sandboy
as hungry as a hunter
as ignorant as a child

as innocent as a babe
as little as Tom Thumb
as mad as a hatter
as mean as a miser
as pale as a ghost
as pleased as Punch
as sober as a judge
as strong as Hercules/Samson
as tall as a giant
as thick as thieves
as white as a ghost

as strong as Hercules/Samson

Below is a list of nouns that are also used when describing people. These need not be used with **like** or **as**; e.g. Leslie is a **wizard** at mathematics.

an angel a person who is gentle and kind to others
a devil a particularly wicked or mischievous person
a giant a person who is very large
a saint a person who leads a very holy life
a wizard a clever and skilful person
an Adonis a very handsome man
an Apollo a man with a perfect physique or body shape
a Goliath an extremely large man
a Hercules a very strong man
a Judas a mean traitor
a Samson a very strong man
a Solomon a very wise man

2. Similes based on the Distinctive Qualities of Other Living Things

as agile as a monkey
as angry as a wasp
as big as an elephant
as blind as a bat
as bold as a lion
as brave as a lion
as bright as a lark
as busy as a bee/ant/beaver
as calm as a cat
as clumsy as a bear
as crafty as a fox
as cunning as a fox
as faithful as a dog

as big as an elephant

as graceful as
a swan

as fast as a deer/hare
as fat as a pig/whale
as fierce as a tiger
as friendly as a puppy
as frisky as a lamb
as gay as a lark
as gentle as a lamb/dove
as graceful as a swan
as hairy as a gorilla
as happy as a lark
as harmless as a dove
as heavy as an elephant
as hungry as a wolf
as lazy as a toad
as lively as a cricket
as meek as a lamb
as mischievous as a monkey
as nervous as a mouse
as patient as an ox
as persistent as a mosquito
as playful as a kitten/puppy
as plump as a partridge

as poor as a church mouse
as powerful as a lion
as proud as a peacock
as quiet as a lamb/mouse
as red as a turkey-cock
as serious as an owl
as sick as a dog
as silly as a goat/goose/sheep
as slippery as an eel/a serpent
as slow as a snail/tortoise
as sly as a fox
as strong as an ox/a horse
as stubborn as a mule
as stupid as an ass/a donkey
as sure-footed as a goat
as swift as an eagle/a deer/hare/hawk
as tender as (a) chicken
as timid as a mouse
as ugly as a toad
as weak as a kitten
as wise as an owl

as proud as a peacock

135

As with group 1. above, animal words can also be used as nouns and adjectives to describe people, without the use of **like** or **as**.

Nouns:

an ape a person who foolishly imitates others
an ass/donkey a stupid person
a bear a clumsy, rough person
a cat a spiteful, 'catty' person (usually referring to females)
a dog a worthless person; someone who is despised
an elephant a huge, clumsy, ungainly person

a fox a crafty, cunning person
a goose a silly person
a lamb an innocent, harmless person
a monkey a child who is full of mischievous tricks
a mule a very stubborn person
a parasite a person who lives off another
a parrot a person who learns things off by heart without understanding
     the real meaning
a pest a troublesome person; one who annoys and 'pesters' others
a pig a greedy and dirty person
a snake/serpent a treacherous, dangerous person
a shark a greedy and cunning person; one who swindles others
a snake/serpent a treacherous, dangerous person
a wolf a greedy and cunning person

Adjectives:

canine like a dog
catlike (steps) stealthy steps, noiseless
cattish/catty spiteful; malicious
dogged stubborn
feline like a cat
foxy crafty, cunning
sheepish uncomfortable; embarrassed or ashamed
tigerish fierce

3. Similes based on the Distinctive Qualities of Objects/Things

as ancient as the sun/stars
as beautiful as a rainbow
as black as coal/soot
as bold as brass
as bright as a button/a new penny
as brittle as glass
as brown as a berry
as changeable as the weather
as cheap as dirt
as clean as a new pin
as clear as crystal/daylight/a bell
as cold as ice/marble
as common as dirt
as cool as a cucumber
as crisp as new bank notes

as beautiful as a rainbow

as dark as a dungeon/as midnight
as dead as a doornail/wood
as deaf as a post
as deep as a well
as dry as a bone/as dust
as dull as ditch water/lead
as easy as A.B.C./as pie
as fair as a rose
as fast as light
as fit as a fiddle
as flat as a pancake
as free as the breeze
as fresh as dew/a daisy/a rose/a sea breeze
as good as gold
as green as grass
as hairless as an egg
as hard as iron/nails/marble/stone
as heavy as lead
as hollow as a drum
as honest as a mirror
as hot as a furnace/an oven/as pepper
as immortal as the stars
as invisible as the air
as lasting as the pyramids
as light as a feather/as air
as like as two peas (in a pod)

as loud as thunder
as monotonous as the sea
as new as day
as old as the hills
as opposite as the poles
as pale as death
as pretty as a picture
as pure as a lily
as quick as lightning/a flash
as red as a cherry/a rose
as rotten as an egg
as round as an orange/a ball/a barrel
as safe as houses
as sharp as a razor/needle
as silent as the grave
as smooth as velvet/glass
as soft as butter
as sour as vinegar/lime
as steady as a rock
as still as a statue
as straight as an arrow
as sure as death
as sweet as honey
as swift as an arrow/the wind
as tall as a steeple/mast
as thin as a rake
as thirsty as a sponge
as tough as leather
as transparent as glass
as warm as wool
as white as snow/wool/ivory/a sheet
as yellow as saffron/sulphur

as still as a statue

3   Verbs and Nouns which Idiomatically Go Together

1. English has many expressions in which certain nouns and verbs go together. For example:

> a man may *climb* a mountain, *dig* a garden, *read* a book, *pay* a bill, *save* money. Water, on the other hand, *runs*, *freezes*, *moistens* earth, *feeds* plants.

Below is a sample list of certain verbs with some of the nouns that can follow them:

Break a stick, glass, a rope, a lock; a promise, a treaty, the law; the silence, the peace; one's fast; break one's back, leg, arm, neck, etc.

Catch fish; a ball, a bird, a thief; cold, fever; an infection; a tune; catch one's eye, ear; catch a glimpse of; catch a train, etc.

Draw a cart, a load, a tooth, a bow, a curtain; a line, a figure, a picture; blood, breath, water; tears, groans, a long face; a cheque, interest, a will; draw money from the bank; a conclusion, a moral, an inference, etc.

Give gifts; help; a ride, a drive, a price, a prize; medicine, a drink; an opinion, judgement; praise, thanks, offence; the alarm, a hint, notice, warning, a scolding, a shock; an answer, a reply; give trouble, evidence, permission, powers; give a shout, etc.

Have possessions—a house, a car, talents, powers, authority; room; an appointment, riches, influence, patience, health, hope, beauty, time, a good figure, a wish; a good understanding; a cold, a fever; an interest in, a regard for; have work to do, etc.

Keep goods, money; a secret, a promise; the silence, the peace; guard, watch; a book, a fast; a horse, sheep; keep boarders; keep house; keep a school, shop; keep company with; keep one's ground, footing; keep hold of a thing; keep pace with; keep an eye on; keep in mind; keep a sharp look-out, etc.

Make a speech, a promise, a request, a remark; a fuss, a row, a noise; a will; a record, a copy; a complaint, an effort, an attempt, an experiment, an engagement/appointment; a road, a railway, a journey; a bargain; an offer; friends, progress; make way; make faces; make music; peace, amends; make a fool of, fun of, make haste; make a rush for; make use of; make money, profit; make a choice of; make love to a person; make ends meet; make one's appearance; make a name for oneself; make one happy, miserable; make a bed; etc.

Take by the hand – a pen, a brush; a seat, a walk, a drive; a photograph; steps, precautions, measures, trouble, revenge, satisfaction, control, food, poison, medicine; take a course; time, warning, advice; leave, shape; aim, captive; a fancy to; a liking for; credit for, pleasure in; pride in, charge of, care; the place of, advantage of, possession of, the part of; an interest in, etc.

2. Animals and people, too, are associated with certain noises and movements. In such cases, the name of the animal or person (the noun) and its paired noise or movement (the verb) form an idiomatic expression: e.g.

Sounds made by people:

babies gurgle, coo, cry, weep, scream

people chuckle, giggle, cry, talk, sing, whistle, weep, sob, laugh, shout, snore, etc.

Sounds made by animals:

bears growl

bees hum

birds sing, chirp, whistle, twitter, warble

cats purr, mew

cocks crow

cows moo

dogs bark, growl, howl, yelp, whine, snarl

ducks quack

elephants trumpet

flies buzz

frogs croak

geese cackle, hiss, gobble

goats bleat

hens cackle, cluck

horses neigh, snort, whinny

lambs bleat

lions roar

mice squeak

monkeys chatter, gibber

pigs grunt, squeal

snakes hiss

tigers growl, roar

Sounds made by objects:

aeroplanes drone, zoom

bells (small) ring, tinkle, jingle

bells (large) toll, peal, chime

bombs explode

brakes screech

cameras click

clocks tick, chime

clouds thunder

coins jingle, ring

doors slam, bang

drums beat, roll

engines throb, purr, chug

feet shuffle, tramp (marching), stamp (in anger)

fire crackles

footsteps sound

glasses clink, tinkle

gongs beat, clang

guns boom, roar

hands clap, slap, smack, whack

hearts beat, throb

hinges creak

hoofs clatter, thunder

horns honk, hoot, toot

kettles sing

keys jingle, clink

leaves rustle, crackle

lids (of boxes) slam, bang

loudspeakers blare

plates clatter, crash

propellers (of aeroplanes) whirr

pens scratch

pots and pans clang

radio and TV sets blare

raindrops patter

rivers gurgle

sails flap (in the wind)

shoes (new) squeak

sirens wail

spoons, forks, etc. clatter

steam hisses

teeth chatter (in the cold)

telephones ring, buzz

thunder rumbles, claps, crashes

tyres screech

typewriters clack

twigs snap
vehicles rumble, roar
watches tick
water drips, splashes

waves lap, splash, roar
whistles blow, shriek
(the) wind howls, sighs

4 Idiomatic Adjective Phrases

There are many idiomatic expressions in English that comprise an adjective (or *-ing* participle) and a preposition. Below is a sample of such idiomatic adjective phrases:

accompanied by (a friend)
according to (the plans)
accurate in (his calculations)
accused of (a crime) by (a person)
accustomed to (hard work)
acquainted with (your sister)
acquitted of (the charge)
addicted to (drugs)
adjacent to (his office)
afraid of (ghosts)
angry with (a person); at (a thing); because of (a thing)
annoyed at (a thing); with (a person)
anxious about, for (his results)
ashamed of (himself)
associated with (that business)
astonished at (your enthusiasm)
attentive to (the teacher)
aware of (your intention)
belonging to (that man)
born of (parents); in/at (a place)
busy at/with (her knitting)

capable of (understanding)
careful of (her figure)
careless about (the risks)
certain of (success)
close to/by (my house)
clumsy at (needlework)
complain of (the noise)
composed of (H_2O and O_2)
concerned about (a thing); for (a person)
confident of (success)
conscious of (her absence)
content with (little)
contrary to (opinion)
convenient for (me); to (come)
corresponding to/with (a thing)
crushed to (death)
cured of (a disease)
delighted with (the gift)
dependent on (his parents)
different from (his brother)
disappointed in (someone); with (the offer)
disgusted at (the sight); with (life)
due to (a fire)
eligible for (a scholarship)
envious of (his neighbour)
exempt from (taxation)
expert at (accounts); in (hunting)

141

faithful to (his master)
familiar to/with (a person)
famous for (its batik)
fond of (sweets)
free from (danger)
friendly to (me)
full of (hope)
good at (English); for (business)
guilty of (murder)
hidden by (a friend); from (view)
hopeful of (success)
ignorant of (religion)
impatient at (the delay); for her
    arrival); of (control)
important to (your job)
impressed with (his skill)
incapable of (lying)
indebted to (a person); for
    (a thing)
informed of (his movements)
inhabited by (islanders)
innocent of (the crime)
interested in (your trade)
involved with (a person); in
    (business)
irritated at (a disappointment);
    by (being kept waiting);
    with (my son)
jealous of (his wife)
kind to (the poor)
loyal to (the government)
mad with (rage)

married to (her sister)
obedient to (his mother)
occupied with (work)
opposite to (the bank)
painful to (me)
popular with (his regiment)
praised for (his poetry)
previous/prior to (your arrival)
proficient in (the language)
proud of (his son)
relevant to (the question)
responsible for (a thing); to
    (a person)
satisfied with (his conduct)
short of (money)
sick of (waiting)
similar to (that stamp)
sorry for (his failure)
starve to (death); with
    (cold)
successful in (business)
suitable for (using)
surprised at (his action); by (her
    appearance)
surrounded by (his friends)
suspicious of (a person)
thankful to (a person); for
    (a benefit)
tired of (doing nothing)
unfit for (eating)
useful to (a person); for (a
    purpose)

5 Idiomatic Prepositional Phrases

Although prepositions form a small class of words in English (See page 85) they frequently combine with other word classes to form a large number of idiomatic expressions. As with other idioms, the order of the words in the phrase is fixed and, if altered, will give a different meaning to the phrase.

Below is a sample of common prepositions used in a number of idiomatic expressions:

About: about five o'clock; about three kilometres; a discussion about; to talk about; to travel about town

Above: above someone's head; to rise above the clouds; a man above suspicion; to live above one's means; a thing done above-board = something done openly

Across: across the street; a bridge across a river; a road across the desert; to walk across a field

After: after lunch; after 5 o'clock; after two hours; to come day after day; after dark

Against: against the rules, law; against orders; to go against the wind, the tide, the current; to vote against a motion; to go against someone; to work against time

Along: along the beach, the valley, the highway

Among (st): among friends; to hide among the grass, trees; among the people

Around: around the world, country

At: at noon, at daybreak; at Easter/Christmas/New Year; at fault; at liberty; at leisure; at school, at university; at full speed; at home; at the door; at a distance; at any rate; at a standstill; at first sight; at a dollar (a metre); to be at large

Before: before one's eyes, face; to appear before someone; to do something before breakfast, lunch, noon, night

Behind: behind one's back; behind a cloud; behind a door; behind time; behind you; to leave nothing behind

Below: below the stairs, table, etc.; below average; below the rank of a . . .; to hit below the belt; below standard height

Beneath: beneath notice, contempt, dignity

Beside: (= by the side of) beside the wall, a fire; beside a person

Besides: (= in addition to) besides all this; to have something besides something else

Between: between friends; between ourselves; between morning and night; between the hours of two and five; between this and the end of the month; war between two countries; a distance between two places; a misunderstanding/quarrel between two persons

Beyond: beyond limits; beyond the sea, the stars; the village; beyond doubt; beyond expectation; beyond reach; beyond one's income

By: by force; by chance; to travel by land, water, air; to go by rail, ship; to read by the light of a lamp; by fits and starts; a pump driven by water, wind, steam, etc.; to be by oneself; to know someone by name; to receive a letter by post; to be taken by surprise; to learn by heart; destroy by fire, a flood, an earthquake; by noon, by nightfall; by his side; to sell by the metre, by the dozen, by the ounce; to do things by halves; to sit side by side

Down: downstairs; down the stairs, the hill, the river; to look down; to go down

During: a ruler's reign; a battle; a lifetime; the holidays

For: something for someone; a house for sale; to be ill for a week; for a time; to look for help; to leave for school, the office; to know for certain; to sell for money; to flee for one's life; to be left for dead; to go for a walk, jog, ride; to work for money, fame, praise; to read for information, enjoyment; to fight for one's life; tit for tat

From: away from home; far from home; to receive something from a person, place; safe from danger; free from worry; from childhood, from youth; from experience; released from jail; rescued from danger; free from fear; authority from the government, etc.; saved from drowning; separate the good from the bad; to rise from the ranks; from first to last; from door to door; from side to side; from hand to mouth; from bad to worse

In: in the room, house, hall, etc.; in parliament, in court; in danger; in his presence/absence; in the distance; in the background; in heaven; in the sun, in the open air, in the dark; in a corner; walk in front; in summer, winter, etc.; just in time; in difficulty; in haste; in a deep sleep; to talk in a whisper; to walk in silence; to pay in advance; the work in hand; to be in love with; to be in debt; keep in mind; work in harmony; in the end; put in order.

Into: come into the room, house, garden; fall into the water; let into a secret; to look into a matter; pour water into a vase, jug, etc.; to get into difficulty

Near: near a fire, a door; near one's parents; to be near the mountains, the seaside; to be near death

Of: a herd of cattle, etc.; a crown of gold; the capital of a country; a native of a place; the people of a place; a matter of course; of use; of value; of importance; a course of medicine; a course of physics; a place of honour; a Bachelor of Arts; the price of things; the force of the wind, sand, water; hard of hearing; of necessity; to have the right of way; to be short of money, food; to cure someone of an illness; etc.

Off: off the coast, the mainland; to fall off something; to catch someone off guard; to be off work; to do something off-hand

On: on land; on board; on the table, floor, etc.; on the roof; on the road; to play on an instrument; to go on foot, horseback; to be on

144

good behaviour; goods on sale; on an average; a house on fire; on the one hand; on each side; on a public occasion; to pay on demand; to have pity on someone; on the move; to stand on tiptoe; his hair stood on end; to be on duty; on trial

Out of: out of use; out of favour; out of reach; out of the way; out of step; out of place; out of fashion; out of date; out of order; out of tune; out of print; out of doors; out of hearing; out of danger; out of fear; out of breath; out of one's depth

Over: over the hills, the town; over the country; to look over one's shoulder; to have advantages over another; to fall head over heels (in love); to stay overnight; to show someone over a house

Past: past hope; past cure; past recovery; past feeling; past control; past 3 o'clock; past our help

Round: a trip round the world; a fence round the house; a walk round the garden

Through: through the door, gate; through the wood; through the water; through the ages; to go through difficult times; to go through thick and thin; all through the year; through life; to look through a book; to get something through influence

To: to a house, etc.; roads go to places; go to bed; give something to someone; pray to God; beaten to death; sweet to the taste; pleasing to the eye; to keep a secret to oneself; from first to last; from day to day; from time to time; from beginning to end

Under: under a tree; under the house; underground; underwater; undercover; under arrest; under sentence of death; a matter under discussion, consideration; to act under orders; to speak under one's breath; under an impression; under suspicion; to be under age; under foot; under one's feet; under lock and key

Up: to go upstairs; to walk up a hill; to swim up the river; to go up-country

Upon: something upon a table; upon his word; to stand upon one's rights; once upon a time; upon occasion; upon consideration

With: to go with someone; to travel with someone; to make something with an implement/tool; walk with haste; to pass an examination with credit/distinction; side by side with

Within: within reach; within range; within easy distance; within the target; within the month; within a mile; within an hour; to live within one's income; keep within doors

Without: to escape without harm, damage; to be without help; without success; to be without hope; to come without fail; come without delay; to act without thinking; to be without a child, husband, a home

Some prepositional phrases consist of a preposition and a noun followed by another preposition:

at the end of	in front of	on the eve of
at the side of	in honour of	on the part of
at the top of (one's voice)	in hope of	on the point of
	in order to	out of proportion with/to
because of	in place of	under the name of
by means of	in search of	with a view to
by the side of	in spite of	with an eye to
for fear of	instead of	with reference to
for the purpose of	in the event of	with regard to
for the sake of	in the face of	with respect to
in case of	in the hope of	with the help of
in common with	in view of	with the hope of
in connexion with	on account of	with the intention of
in favour of	on behalf of	

6 Verbs followed Idiomatically by Prepositions

Certain verbs when followed by certain prepositions have a different meaning than when the verb stands alone:

Break :	break away	to free oneself; get away
	break into	enter forcibly
	break off	to stop; separate
	break open	open with force
	break out	to appear suddenly; to escape
	break up	to break in pieces; to come to an end
	break with	stop being friendly with

It is important to choose the correct preposition for a particular verb in order to express what you mean. Below is a sample list of verbs followed by prepositions. As it is not a complete listing, it is wise to consult a good dictionary when in doubt as to which preposition to use.

accuse of (an offence)

agree on (the purchase); agree to (do something); agree with (someone)

146

aim at (an animal); aim for (a place)
apologize to (a person) for (a thing)
apply to (a person) for (a job)
approve of (an application)
argue with (a person); argue for *or* against *or* about (a thing)
arrive at (a place) in (a vehicle) from (a place)
ask about (a thing); ask after (a person); ask for (a thing)
bargain with (someone) for (something)
belong to (someone)
blame for (something)
boast of (something)
care for (a person, thing); care about (something)
close down (a business)
come by (bus)
compare to (something); compare with (a person, thing)
compete with (a person) for (a thing)
complain of (a thing) to (a person); complain against/of (a person)
cope with (a task)
correspond with (a person) about (a thing)
decide on (an action); against/for (an action)
depend on (someone) for (something)
disagree with (someone) on/about (something)
disapprove of (something)
distinguish between (two things); distinguish from (one another)
divide between (two persons); among (more than two persons)
enter into (an agreement)
escape from (a place)
excel in (a subject)
exchange (a thing) with (a person) for (something)
explain (a thing) to (a person)
fight against (a country) for (one's life) with (a weapon)
hand in (an application); hand out/over (something) to (someone)
hint at (something)
hope for (something)
inquire into (a matter); inquire of (a person);
    inquire about/after (something)
insist on (something)
invest in (a thing); invest (a person) with (a title)
live with (someone) at (a place) in (a country)
long for (a person, a thing)
meet with (a person, an accident)
object to (something)

part from (a person); part with (something)
prefer (something) to (something else)
prevent (someone) from (doing something)
protest against (something)
provide for (someone)
punish (a person) for (an ill deed)
quarrel with (a person) over/about (something)
rebel against (authority, a person)
recover from (an illness)
refer to (a dictionary, etc.)
rely on (a person) for (help)
reply to (a letter)
rescue from (danger)
result from (a cause); result in (an effect)
retire from (a job)
search for (a thing, a person lost)
see about (a matter)
separate from (something)
speak on (a topic); speak of/about (a matter); speak with (a person)
stand against (someone else); stand for (election)
subscribe to (a magazine)
suffer from (an illness)
supply (someone) with (something)
think of (a person, thing); think over (a problem)
threaten (someone) with (something)
trade in (something) with (someone, a country)
trust in/to (someone, something); trust with (money)
vote for/against (a motion)
warn (someone) of (something)
watch for (someone, something); watch over (someone)
wish for (something)
work on/at (a project) with (someone)

The verbs below are followed by numerous prepositions and adverbs. Do you know the differences in meaning between them?

Get about, above, ahead, along, among, at, away, back, before, behind, between, beyond, down, forward, in, into, near, off, on, on with, over, out, round, through, to, up

Go about, abroad, across, after, against, ahead, along with, aside, at, away, back, between, beyond, by, down, for, forth, in, in for, into, off, on, on with, out, out of, over, through, through with, to, up, up and down, up to, upon, with, without

Look about, after, at, away, back, down on, for, forward, forward to, in, into, on, out, out for, out of, over, through, to, up, up to

Put away, back, by, down, forward, in, in at, in for, off, on, out, over, up, up to, up with

Run after, against, at, away, away from, away with, down, in, into, off, on, out, over, through, to, up

Take after, away, back, by, down, for, from, in, off, on, out, over, to, up, up with, upon oneself

7   Idiomatic Adverbial Phrases

Two or more adverbs can be joined together to form an idiomatic phrase. It is important to note that the order of each of the adverbs is fixed.

again and again repeatedly; continually; very often: She asked her son *again and again* to study for his exams.

back and forth/backwards and forwards moving first in one direction and then in the opposite direction (one or more times): The lion walked *backwards and forwards* in its cage.

by and by before long; soon: She'll return home *by and by*.

by and large on the whole; in general; all things considered: *By and large* his work is excellent.

far and away very much: He is *far and away* the best student in the form.

far and near/far and wide everywhere: Visitors came to the wedding from *far and near/far and wide*.

first and foremost firstly; in the first place: *First and foremost*, I disapprove of his going overseas when he is so young.

here and there scattered about; in various places: He is a very untidy boy; he always leaves his things *here and there*.

149

here, there and everywhere everywhere; in all possible places: I looked *here, there and everywhere* for my pen but I still couldn't find it.

in and out sometimes inside and sometimes outside: She's been *in and out* of hospital for the last five years.

more or less (a) almost; nearly; (b) about; not exactly: The painting's *more or less* finished; The repairs to my motor bike cost *more or less* a hundred dollars.

now and again not very often; sometimes; occasionally: We go to see a play *now and again*.

(every) now and then/again at times; from time to time: *Every now and then* I think of my time at university.

off and on/on and off from time to time; occasionally; irregularly: He looks for a job *off and on* but most of the time he's happy to stay at home.

on and on without stopping: He talked *on and on* without giving anyone else a chance to talk.

once or twice a few times; several times: *Once or twice* I've studied in the library but I prefer to study at home.

once and for all finally; for the last time; now but never again: *Once and for all*, did you take my purse?

out and away by far; much: He's *out and away* the funniest person I know.

out and out complete; thorough; total: She's an *out and out* believer in ghosts.

over and over (again) repeatedly; again and again; very often: I've told her *over and over again* that she's not to stay out late at night.

round and round repeatedly or continually moving round: The bird flew *round and round* looking for its babies.

through and through completely; entirely; in every way: She's like her mother *through and through*, even the way she talks.

to and fro backwards and forwards; from side to side: The teacher walked *to and fro* in front of the class as he read the poem.

up and about on one's feet; up again after an illness: My father was *up and about* two weeks after his operation.

8 Groups of Idiomatic Expressions

In English there are sets or groups of common idiomatic expressions that belong to particular subjects, for example, money, business, buying and selling, warfare, letters, clocks and watches, time, sight, the sea, ships, fire, light, health, death. To get to know and understand such groups of expressions, it is necessary to consult a dictionary or a book of idioms. However, listed below are samples of such groupings of idioms.

1. Expressions based on Parts of the Body

to backbite a person to speak ill of someone
to back chat to be cheeky; to talk back to someone
to be a bag of bones to be extremely thin
to be a blockhead to be an idiot; a fool
to be a great hand at (something) to be an expert; skilled
to be a sight for sore eyes someone or something who appears before another and is very welcome
to be all ears to be eager to listen
to be armed to the teeth fully armed or protected
to be at one's wits' end completely puzzled; not knowing what to do next
to be close-fisted to be mean; miserly
to be double-faced to be two-faced; insincere
to be down in the mouth to feel depressed and unhappy
to be head and shoulders above someone else to be very much better or superior
to be out of one's mind to be mad; crazy
to be someone's blue-eyed boy to be someone's favourite; to do no wrong in someone else's eyes
to be the apple of someone's eye to be someone's favourite; much-loved
to bite someone's head off to speak abruptly or sharply to another
to burn one's fingers to get into trouble
to catch someone's eye to suddenly exchange glances with another
to change hands to pass from one owner to another
to cut someone's throat to charge him a very high price
to dig someone in the ribs to make unkind remarks or insinuations about another
to eat one's heart out (for another) to long for someone who is unattentive
to feel something in one's bones to have a feeling or premonition about something
to foot the bill to pay the bill (especially for some social outing)
to get on someone's nerves to irritate someone very greatly
to get something off one's chest to confess to something; to unburden oneself

151

to get the upper hand to gain mastery over an opponent

to give someone the cold shoulder to ignore someone; to slight another

to give someone the sharp edge of one's tongue to thoroughly scold another person

to go on all hands to crawl on hands and knees

to have a bone to pick with someone to argue with someone over a particular issue

to have a chip on one's shoulder to bear a grudge against the world/society

to have a finger in every pie to have many (business) interests

to have a head like a sieve to have a very poor memory; very forgetful

to have a skeleton in the cupboard to have a guilty secret (especially a family scandal)

to have a skeleton in the cupboard

to have at one's fingertips to know thoroughly

to have bags under the eyes to have soft, dark skin under the eyes

to have cold feet to be afraid

to have no backbone to be a weak, spineless person

to have one's head screwed on to be very sensible

to have something/someone on the brain to think constantly about something/someone

to have someone under one's thumb to dominate another; to control them

to have the upper hand to be in command/charge; to be someone in power

to have two left hands someone who is clumsy; drops things

to hold one's tongue to keep silent even though there is an urge to talk

to hold up one's head to be able to look people in the face; not ashamed

to jump out of one's skin to get a sudden fright

to keep a cool head to keep calm (especially in an emergency)

to keep a stiff upper lip to remain courageous and calm

to keep one's eye on something to watch; pay attention to

to keep one's fingers crossed to hope for luck

to keep one's hair on to keep cool and patient

to keep one's head above water to avoid getting into debt or trouble

to keep one's nose out of to not interfere in someone's affairs

to keep someone at arm's length not too friendly with another; stand-offish

to keep someone
at arm's length

to keep someone's nose to the grindstone to make someone work very hard and constantly

to knock something on the head to suddenly stop an idea/project

to know something by heart to be able to say something from memory

to laugh on the other side of one's face to experience disappointment after expecting success

to lay hands on someone to handle someone roughly

to lend a hand to help

to let the grass grow under one's feet to be inactive and uninvolved

to live from hand to mouth to live in hardship with the barest essentials

to look as if butter wouldn't melt in one's mouth to look very innocent

to lose face to lose one's honour/reputation

to lose heart to be discouraged

to lose one's head to lose control of oneself; to be very angry

to make a clean breast of something to confess to something; to reveal all

to make neither head nor tail of something to understand nothing of a particular issue

to make someone's mouth water to cause to want (usually food)

to palm someone off with something to make someone buy something they don't really want

to pat someone on the back to give praise and encouragement to another

to pay through the nose for something to pay an overly high price for something

to poison someone's mind to turn someone against another person

to pull one's weight to do one's share of work

to pull someone's leg to play a joke on someone

to pull the wool over someone's eyes to deceive another

to put one's back into it to work hard; to work in earnest

to put one's foot down to be firm about an issue; to insist firmly

to put one's foot in it to say or do something very tactless; to get into trouble

to put one's shoulder to the wheel to work hard and earnestly

to put someone's nose out of joint to make someone jealous by taking his place as the centre of attraction

they put their heads together to work with someone else to solve a problem

to rack one's brains to try to recall or remember something

to receive with open arms to welcome warmly

to save face to save one's honour/reputation/name

to show a clean pair of heels to escape by running

to snap someone's head off to speak abruptly

to speak one's mind to be frank and honest

to split hairs to make subtle and useless distinctions

to stand on one's own legs/feet to do things without help; to be independent

to sweep someone off his feet to flatter and woo someone (usually a girl)

to take matters into one's own hands to do something independently without help

to take something to heart to take something seriously

to take to one's heels to run away

to throw dust in someone's eyes to try to deceive someone

to tread in someone's footsteps to follow the example of another (usually of talent/occupation)

to tread on someone's toes to offend another person

to try one's hand at to try doing something for the first time

to turn a blind eye (to) to refuse to see

to turn a deaf ear to refuse to hear

to tread on
someone's toes

to turn one's head to make conceited
to turn up one's nose at something to treat with contempt
to twist someone's arm to force someone into doing something for you
to twist someone round one's little finger to manipulate someone for
   your own desires
to wash one's hands of something to have nothing to do with a particular matter

2. Expressions based on Colours

(an agreement) in black and white (an agreement) in writing or print
black and blue badly bruised after a fall/a beating
a blacklist a list of people, groups, countries, etc. who have done something wrong (and who will be punished in some way)
a black mark a record showing that one has done some wrong
black market illegal sale of goods that are difficult to obtain
black Monday the day children go back to school after their holidays
to black out to lose consciousness for a short while
a black sheep a bad character who disgraces his family
in someone's black books out of favour with someone
to blackmail someone to threaten to reveal someone's misdeeds unless
   he pays money
blue blood royal or noble blood
a blue-collar job a factory job; a job requiring little skill
a bolt from the blue a complete surprise
to feel blue/have the blues to be sad or depressed
once in a blue moon only occasionally; very rarely
out of the blue suddenly; without warning
to scream blue murder to complain loudly
the green-eyed monster jealousy

155

to have green fingers/a green thumb to have a natural skill in making plants grow well

a greengrocer a person who sells fruit and vegetables

a greenhorn an inexperienced person

the green light the signal to proceed; to go ahead

green with envy filled with jealousy

a greybeard an old man

grey matter brains; common sense

(to be) in the pink of health to be in excellent health

purple with rage so angry that the face becomes purple

to be caught red-handed caught in the act of committing a crime

a red carpet welcome a special ceremonial welcome to a guest

the red flag a flag used as a danger signal

a red-letter day a notable, fortunate day that will be remembered

the red light a signal to stop; a danger signal

to paint the town red to go out and get drunk and behave noisily

the Reds the Communists

red tape official rules which cause delay in settling one's problems

to see red to lose control of oneself in anger

a white-collar job an office job; indoor work

a white elephant a worthless possession which the owner wants to get rid of

the white flag a sign that one accepts defeat or surrenders

to show the white feather to show signs of cowardice

yellow at heart cowardly

to be/feel off colour to be unwell or rather ill

to change colour to turn pale

to come off with flying colours to achieve great success

to have a high colour to appear very red in the face

to show one's true colours to show what one is really like; one's true character

9 Idiomatic Verbal Expressions

to act the goat to behave foolishly or childishly

to air one's opinion to express one's feelings in public

to be a chip off the old block a son who is very much like his father in appearance, character, habits, etc.

to be as fit as a fiddle to be in excellent health; very active

to be at a loose end to have nothing to do

156

to be at the end of one's tether

to be at a loss for words to be speechless; not knowing what to say

to be at death's door to be so ill as to be near death

to be at sixes and sevens to be in confusion and discord

to be at the end of one's tether to be at a loss as to what to do; unable to proceed farther

to be born under a lucky star to have considerable luck in whatever one does

to be born with a silver spoon in one's mouth to be born into a rich family

to be dead beat to be worn out by fatigue

to be in hot water to be in serious trouble

to be in someone's bad/good books to be out of/in favour with someone

to be in the dog-house to be out of favour with someone

to be in the doldrums to be in low spirits; depressed; very unhappy

to be in the same boat to have the same troubles/circumstances

to be like a bear with a sore head to be very bad-tempered; grumpy

to be mad about someone to like someone very much

to be made of money to be well-off; to have plenty of money

to be on tenterhooks to be in a state of suspense and anxiety

to be on the ball to be alert, up-to-date, prepared

to be on the horns of a dilemma not knowing what to do from several courses of action

to be on the rocks to be in danger of failing, collapse (especially a business, a marriage)

to be on top of the world to be very happy; in high spirits

to be out of the question something not worth discussing or considering

to be out of the woods to be out of danger (especially a serious illness)

to be quick on the uptake to be alert and quick to do or say something

to be rolling in money to be rich; to have plenty of money

to be rooted to the spot unable to move (usually through fear)

to be scared to death to be extremely frightened of something

to be short of money not having very much money; not enough money

to be slow on the uptake slow to do or say something

to be tied to (his) mother's apron strings to be under the control and influence of his mother

to be tied to his mother's apron strings

to be too big for one's boots to think very highly of oneself

to bear the brunt of to bear the main force or strain of some action

to beat about the bush to be indecisive; not coming to the point

to bet one's bottom dollar to be absolutely certain about something

to blow hot and cold to do one thing at one time and the opposite soon after

to blow one's own trumpet to boast about one's abilities, achievements

to bore someone stiff/to tears to disinterest a listener with one's talk

to break the ice to take the first step; to be the first to begin (especially a conversation)

to bring down the house to cause loud and long applause through one's skill (e.g. musical talents)

to bring to light to disclose, reveal

to build castles in the air to daydream; to think of things impossible to realize

to burn a hole in the pocket money that is quickly spent

to burn the candle at both ends to use one's energy in two directions at the same time

to burn the midnight oil to work till late at night

to bury the hatchet to make peace; forget past quarrels

to call a spade a spade to speak out bluntly and frankly

to carry a thing too far to continue beyond what is wise or safe

to catch at a straw to grasp at something trifling when in difficulties

to change one's tune to change one's opinion about something

to clip one's wings to deprive one of power and/or freedom

to cook an account to tamper with/falsify an account

to come down on someone like a ton of bricks to harshly criticize another

to come of age to reach adulthood (usually 21 years of age)

to come to grief to meet with disaster

to come to light to become known

to count sheep to try various methods (including counting) to get to sleep

to count sheep

to cry over spilt milk to be unhappy about something that can no longer be remedied

to curry favour to seek/win favour by gifts or flattery

to cut a long story short to shorten a story which would take a long time to tell to listeners

to cut off in its prime to destroy something when it is at its best

to cut one's coat according to one's cloth to live within one's income; to make what one possesses serve one's needs

to cut someone down to size to put someone in his place (especially a person who thinks too highly of himself)

to do a city/the sights to visit a city and see its well-known places

to do a thing by fits and starts to work intermittently, not continuously on something

to do a thing by hook or by crook to do something by any means, fair or foul, direct or indirect

to do something on the spur of the moment to suddenly decide to do something

to draw a line at to refuse to go beyond a certain limit

to drive someone mad/round the bend/up the wall to irritate someone very much with one's behaviour, actions, words

to drop a brick to say or do something very tactless and unexpected

to drop a hint to make veiled and subtle suggestions

to drown one's sorrows to get drunk on alcohol in order to forget one's problems

to eat like a horse to have a hearty appetite; to eat a lot

to eat one's words to apologize; to take back what one has said

to egg on to spur on to further action

to face the music to meet the worst; to face punishment for doing something wrong

to fall out with someone to quarrel with someone

to fall through to fail (especially a plan, project)

to fancy someone/something to take a great liking to

to feather one's nest to provide dishonestly for oneself

to fight like cats and dogs to be constantly quarrelling

to fight shy of to avoid

to fire someone to dismiss someone from employment

to flog a dead horse to try fruitlessly to revive interest in something (e.g. an organization)

to follow the crowd to believe or act as most people do; to follow unthinkingly

to follow suit to do the same thing as another person

to gain ground to make progress in an undertaking

to get a move on to hurry up

to get away with something to escape detection despite doing something wrong

to get blood out of stone to get more than is fair out of someone

to get down to work to start on the task in hand

to get even with someone to take revenge on someone; to do something to them in return for what they've done to you

to get hitched to get married

to get hold of the wrong end of the stick to misunderstand someone or something

to get into a flap/a state to get worried and nervous

to get into hot water to be in/to get into trouble

to get off scot-free to escape punishment; to be let off payment

to get one's (own) way to succeed in doing what one wants to do regardless of the opinion of others

to get out of bed on the wrong side to start the day in a bad temper

to get the sack to be dismissed from some employment

to get wind of to hear a rumour of

to get the wind up to get a fright; to get worried and nervous

to give someone a ring/tinkle to telephone someone

to give someone a telling-off/a ticking-off to scold someone

to give someone the slip to manage to avoid someone who is looking for you

to give the game away to let out a secret

to give up the ghost to cease trying; also, to die

to go a long way to excel; to go far (especially in a career)

to go from bad to worse to deteriorate (especially a situation)

to go off at a tangent to change suddenly to a different course of thought or action

to go like a bomb to function well (especially a vehicle); to go fast

to go out of one's way to take special trouble to help someone

to go to rack and ruin to deteriorate (especially a property); to be unkempt and untidy

to go to the devil/the dogs to not care about one's life, one's actions or appearance; to degenerate

to grin and bear it to put up with something; to make the best of a bad job

to haul (someone) over the coals to scold/reprimand someone

to have a bee in one's bonnet to be strong-minded over certain issues

to have a difference of opinion with someone to have a mild quarrel with someone over something

to have a screw loose to be slightly mad; also, He's not right in the head

to have a soft spot for to be very fond of someone or something (e.g. a place, a type of food)

to have an axe to grind to have a selfish motive for doing something

to have one's knife in someone to be always finding fault with another person

to have one's knife in someone

to hit below the belt to attack an opponent unfairly

to hit the jackpot to win the biggest amount of money to be won in a competition, game of chance, etc.

to hit the nail on the head to do or say exactly the right thing

to hold the purse strings to have control of finance (especially in a family)

to jog someone's memory to remind someone of something

to jump out of the frying-pan into the fire to get out of one bad situation and fall into another, worse situation

to keep a person in the dark to keep something hidden from someone

to keep a thing to oneself not to announce the thing that one knows

to keep open house to encourage visitors to come at any time

to keep one's pecker up to keep one's courage up

to keep one's shirt on to keep cool and calm in a dispute

to keep oneself to oneself to avoid society; to live apart from others

to keep pace with to keep up with (physically and mentally)

to keep the ball rolling to keep a conversation going

to keep the peace to live harmoniously with others

to keep up appearances to pretend to be well-off and to live in a certain style

to kick the bucket to die

to kid someone to tease

to kill two birds with one stone to accomplish two things with one action

to knock off (work) to stop working

to knock someone down with a feather to surprise someone very much

to know the ropes to be thoroughly familiar with a particular situation

to know which side one's bread is buttered to know what is of most benefit for oneself

to kowtow to someone to act in a very servile manner hoping for recognition or favour

to lay down the law to speak in an authoritative way

to lead a charmed life one who passes through great danger without receiving injury

to lead someone a dog's life to give someone a miserable life

to lead someone up the garden path to deceive someone by hiding the real intention

to leave someone in the lurch to desert someone in time of difficulties

to leave the beaten track to travel by a route not commonly used

to leave much to be desired to be unsatisfactory (especially a task done)

to let bygones be bygones to let things that are past and gone remain untouched and forgotten

162

to look for a needle
in a haystack

to let someone down to disappoint another by not fulfilling promises

to let the cat out of the bag to reveal a secret; to expose a trick

to look for a needle in a haystack to begin a search for something with only a small chance of success

to look like a wet week to look miserable and depressed

to lose one's bearings to be unsure of one's direction or position

to make a bee-line for to go straight to

to make a go of something to try one's best to succeed in something

to make a hash/a mess of something to fail at a task; to spoil it

to make a mountain out of a molehill to give great importance to small things

to make a packet/a pile to make a lot of money

to make a pig of oneself to overeat; to be greedy

to make believe to pretend

to make both ends meet to be able to manage on one's income

to make fun of someone or something to laugh at; to joke about

to make hay while the sun shines to take advantage of an opportunity

to make much ado about nothing to make a great fuss about something unimportant

to make one's mouth water food that is delicious; the smell of food makes one want to eat it

to make one's way in the world to succeed in the occupation one chooses; to become successful

to make oneself at home to be comfortable in another's home

to make oneself scarce to disappear; to go off

to make short work of something to do a job very quickly; not wasting time

to make the best of a bad bargain/job to turn a disappointment into an advantage

to make the best/most of a thing to get the greatest advantage from something

to mind one's own business to not meddle or interfere in another's life

to miss a golden opportunity to fail to seize an advantage

to nip something in the bud to stop something before it can develop into something serious

to paddle one's own canoe to tackle one's problems oneself

to paint the town red to have a gay, noisy time

to pass the buck to pass on the responsibility

to pass the hat around to collect money/donations from a group of people

to pave the way to facilitate; make easier

to pay the earth for something to pay an overly-high price for something

to pick a quarrel with someone to provoke someone to an argument/quarrel

to pick holes in something to find fault with; to seek out faults

to pick to pieces to analyse critically

to pick and choose to make a careful selection

to play a double game to do one thing openly and a different thing in secret

to play fast and loose to disregard one's promises

to play second fiddle to take a secondary/subordinate position

to play truant to stay away from (e.g. school)

to play with fire to do something that can lead to serious trouble

to pooh-pooh an idea to express contempt for an idea

to pull one's socks up to make an effort to improve oneself

to pull one's weight to help; to do one's share of work

to pull oneself together to recover one's wits/composure

to pull strings to use friends in influential positions (or to use one's own influence) to secure favours

to put someone in his place to reprimand someone who does not follow correct procedure

to put the cart before the horse to do the wrong thing first; to begin at the wrong end to do something

to put two and two together to arrive at a conclusion; to deduce

to put a spoke in one's wheel to hinder; to obstruct progress

164

to rain cats and dogs

to rain cats and dogs to rain continuously, without stopping
to read between the lines to detect the hidden meaning
to rest on one's laurels to be satisfied with one's achievements
to rule the roost to domineer over others
to run in the blood family characteristics; inherited qualities
to save appearances to present a fair outside; avoid exposure
to screw up/pluck up one's courage to be brave enough to do something
to see something through coloured spectacles to see only the best points about a thing
to see the light to begin to understand
to show a bold front to act bravely in front of others
to sit on the fence to take neither side in a dispute; to remain neutral
to smell a rat to become suspicious about something
to sponge on someone/to cadge something to borrow something, especially money
to spread like wildfire to spread or circulate very quickly
to stand/stick up for to defend, support
to steer clear of to avoid
to stick to one's guns to keep firmly to one's decision
to take advantage of to seize an opportunity
to take a break/a breather to have a short rest
to take a turn for the better/worse to improve/deteriorate in health
to take French leave to be absent from work, etc. without permission
to take great pains with something to do one's best; to do a job very carefully and well; to take a lot of trouble
to take it easy to not worry about work, etc; to live in a leisurely way
to take someone down a peg to put someone in his place; to tell a person what he is really like
to take someone for a ride to deceive; to swindle someone

to take the bull by the horns

to take the bull by the horns to meet a difficulty with courage; to act despite risks

to take the law/matters into one's own hands to punish a person (usually by force) without his being tried in a law court

to take with a pinch of salt to accept what someone has said with doubt and misgiving

to talk nineteen to the dozen to speak a lot; very talkative

to talk the hind legs off a donkey to talk a great deal at great length

to tear a strip off someone to scold harshly; to tell someone off

to throw cold water upon to discourage effort

to throw in the sponge/towel to give up; to admit defeat

to try someone's patience to irritate someone until they have no patience left

to turn over a new leaf to give up one's bad ways and lead a better life

to turn the tables (on someone) to defeat someone who has previously defeated you; to reverse the condition

to upset the apple cart to disturb the routine, the pattern of something

10 Proverbial Phrases

A proverb is a popular saying which expresses a well-known truth or gives a piece of sound advice. Below is a list of the more commonly used proverbs. How many of them do you know?

A bad workman blames his tools.

Absence makes the heart grow fonder.

A bird in the hand is worth two in the bush.

A drowning man will clutch at a straw.

A fool and his money are soon parted.

A friend in need is a friend indeed.

A hungry man is an angry man.

166

All that glitters is not gold.
All's well that ends well.
All work and no play makes Jack a dull boy.
An apple a day keeps the doctor away.
A miss is as good as a mile.
A penny saved is a penny gained.
A rolling stone gathers no moss.
A stitch in time saves nine.
A small leak will sink a great ship.
As the twig is bent so the tree's inclined.
As you made your bed so you must lie in it.
A wild goose never laid a tame egg.
Beggars must not be choosers.
Better late than never.
Birds of a feather flock together.
Blood is thicker than water.
Charity begins at home.
Cut your coat according to your cloth.
Don't carry all your eggs in one basket.
Don't count your chickens before they are hatched.
Don't judge a book by its cover.
Early to bed and early to rise makes a man healthy, wealthy and wise.
Empty vessels make the most noise.
Every cloud has a silver lining.
Every tide has its ebb.
Exchange is no robbery.
Experience teaches fools.
Faint heart never won fair lady.
Fine feathers make fine birds.
Fire is a good servant but a bad master.
First come, first served.
Forbidden fruit tastes sweetest.
Fortune knocks once at every man's door.
God helps those who help themselves.
Great minds think alike.
Greak oaks from little acorns grow.
Half a loaf is better than none.
He who laughs last laughs best.
Honesty is the best policy.
Imitation is the sincerest form of flattery.
It's a long lane that has no turning.
It's never too late to mend.

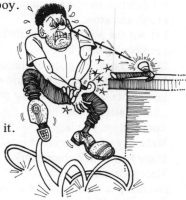

A bad workman blames his tools

Don't count your chickens before they are hatched

167

It's no use crying over spilt milk.
It takes a thief to catch a thief.
It takes two to make a quarrel.
Laugh and grow fat.
Let not the pot call the kettle black.
Let sleeping dogs lie.
Listeners hear no good of themselves.
Little boys should be seen and not heard.
Look after the pence and the pounds will
    look after themselves.
Look before you leap.
Make hay while the sun shines.
Many hands make light work.
More haste, less speed.
Necessity is the mother of invention.
Never put off to tomorrow what you can do today.
New brooms sweep clean.
No news is good news.
No smoke without fire.
Once bitten twice shy.
One good turn deserves another.
One man's meat is another man's poison.
One swallow does not make a summer.
Out of sight, out of mind.
Out of the frying pan and into the fire.
People who live in glass houses shouldn't throw stones.
Practice makes perfect.
Prevention is better than cure.
Robbing Peter to pay Paul.
Rome was not built in a day.
Set a thief to catch a thief.
Shoemakers' wives are worst shod.
Silence gives consent.
Slow and steady wins the race.
Spare the rod and spoil the child.
Speech is silvern, silence is golden.
Strike while the iron is hot.
The least said the soonest mended.
The early bird catches the worm.
Too many cooks spoil the broth.
Two heads are better than one.
When the cat's away the mice will play.

Let sleeping dogs lie

Little boys should be seen
and not heard

168

PART

Vocabulary Building in English

1 **Useful Words for Expressing Ideas, Opinions, etc. in English**

The vocabulary lists below give groups of useful words that can be used to express many ideas in English, for example, expressing personal feelings, opinions. The words are not listed alphabetically; rather, they are grouped according to the similarity of the ideas they express:

1. **Words expressing personal feelings (Nouns)**
   fondness, liking, affection, love
   dislike, hatred
   happiness, joy, delight, gladness
   unhappiness, sadness, misery, depression, sorrow, regret, despair, suffering
   pleasure, satisfaction, contentment, comfort
   pain, dissatisfaction, discontent, discomfort, embarrassment, sympathy, understanding
   enjoyment, amusement, interest, eagerness, excitement, curiosity, surprise, wonder, amazement, astonishment
   dislike, disinterest, boredom, apathy
   disgust, annoyance, exasperation, frustration, worry, concern
   anger, fury, rage
   fear, fright, terror
   tiredness, weariness, exhaustion
   envy, jealousy
   hope—despair   patience—impatience   kindness—meanness
   tolerance—intolerance   friendliness—hostility
   confidence—shyness   appreciation—ingratitude

2. **Words requesting and giving information (Verbs)**
   to ask, to inquire, to request, to question

170

to answer, to respond, to reply
to express, to tell, to inform, to say, to state, to remark, to declare,
to exclaim, to indicate
to hint, to imply
to point out, to announce, to report
to describe, to show, to illustrate, to demonstrate
to discuss, to reveal
to repeat

3. Words expressing the way we think (Verbs)

to think, to know, to believe, to feel, to understand, to consider
to realize, to assume, to suppose
to guess, to imagine, to wonder
to decide, to make up one's mind
to change one's mind, to be confused, to misunderstand
to reason, to define, to deduce, to infer
to compare, to contrast, to interpret
to summarize, to generalize, to theorize, to conclude
to confirm, to verify, to prove, to disprove
to predict, to anticipate

4. Words expressing personal opinions (Verbs)

to be sure, to be convinced, to be certain, to be positive
to be unsure, to be unconvinced, to be uncertain, to be reluctant
to stress, to emphasize, to insist
to agree, to accept
to disagree, to challenge, to reject, to contradict
to argue, to dispute, to object, to oppose
to offer—to refuse
to deny

5. Words concerning making judgements (Verbs)

to be right, to be correct
to be wrong, to be incorrect, to make a mistake
to complain, to criticize
to scold, to blame, to condemn
to promise
to praise, to compliment
to admit, to confess, to apologize, to excuse, to pardon, to forgive
to be innocent—to be guilty
to approve—to disapprove
to judge
to justify

171

6. Words concerning changing other people's behaviour (Verbs)

to persuade, to convince
to suggest, to propose, to advise, to recommend
to invite, to urge
to order, to command, to force, to direct, to demand
to threaten
to forbid, to prohibit
to warn, to caution
to teach, to instruct, to correct
to encourage, to assure, to console, to cheer up
to discourage

2 Single Words for Phrases or Sentences

1. Words referring to number

Referring to one: monogamy, monotonous, unit, union, unity
Referring to two: bicycle, binoculars, bilingual, duel, duet, double, duplicate
Referring to three: tricycle, triangle, trio, triplets, triple, tripod
Referring to four: quarter, quart, quadruped, quadruplets
Referring to more than four:

pentagon	a five-sided figure
hexagon	a six-sided figure
heptagon	a seven-sided figure
octagon	an eight-sided figure
octopus	a sea creature with eight arms

decagon	a ten-sided figure
decade	a period of ten years
decimals	fractions based on tens
decimetre	one-tenth of a metre
century	a period of a hundred years
cent	one-hundredth of a dollar
per cent	out of every hundred
centimetre	one-hundredth of a metre
millimetre	one-thousandth of a metre
millennium	a period of a thousand years
polygon	a figure with more than four sides
polyclinic	a clinic where the doctors treat patients for illness of all parts of the body
polytechnic	a school where many subjects, useful in trades, are taught
polygamy	the custom of having more than one wife at the same time
multiply	to increase in numbers
multitude	a great number of people
multi-coloured	having many colours
multi-storeyed	a building with many storeys/floors
multi-lingual	speaking many languages
multi-racial	of many races

The diagrams on pages 173-4 illustrate some of the words above. Other useful names (of lines and shapes and number) are included.

NUMBERS	WORDS	SYMBOLS
1	decimal point	**1.25**
2	degree	**90°**
3	divided by	÷
4	equals	=
5	fraction	$\frac{1}{2}$
6	minus, subtract	—
7	multiplied by	X
8	per cent	%
9	plus, add	+

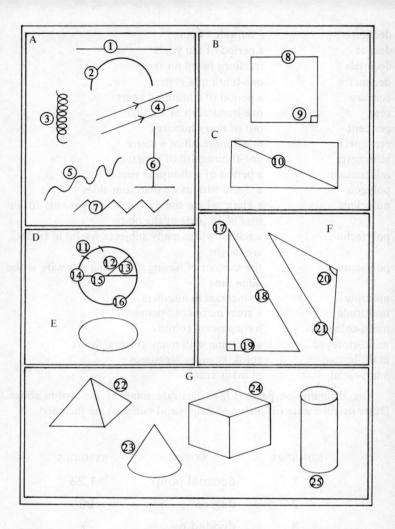

A **LINES**
1 straight line
2 curve
3 spiral
4 parallel lines
5 wavy line
6 perpendicular line
7 zig-zag

B **SQUARE**
8 side
9 right angle

C **RECTANGLE/OBLONG**
10 diagonal

D **CIRCLE**
11 arc
12 radius
13 sector
14 diameter
15 centre
16 circumference

E **OVAL/ELLIPSE**

F **TRIANGLES**
17 apex
18 hypotenuse
19 base
20 obtuse angle
21 acute angle

G **SOLID FIGURES**
22 pyramid
23 cone
24 cube
26 cylinder

174

2. Classification: One name for many things

All things on earth can be divided into two classes or groups:
1. animate (living things), e.g. creatures and plants
2. inanimate (non-living things), i.e. things which are fixed, which cannot eat or move around, e.g. stone, spoon.

It is possible to place every object in a general class either because of its purpose or use or because it resembles other things, e.g. general classes: animals, fishes, insects, vegetables, fruit, occupations, instruments, etc.

The following are useful classification lists:

animal cries	bark, roar, grunt, yelp, bleat
Asians	Chinese, Indians, Thais, Malays, Filipinos
capitals	London, Tokyo, Kuala Lumpur, Paris, Bangkok
colours	crimson, lilac, mauve, beige, maroon, purple
continents	Asia, Africa, Australia, America, Europe
diseases	pneumonia, cholera, typhoid, malaria, cancer
dwellings	house, hut, palace, barracks, hostel
Europeans	The British, Danes, Germans, Italians, Greeks
fabrics	cotton, linen, silk, nylon, tetron
factories	mill, brewery, foundry, workshop
footwear	shoes, boots, slippers, sandals, clogs
fish	tuna, shark, grouper, pomfret, sardine
garments/clothes	shirts, trousers, dresses, blouses, singlets
headwear	hat, cap, helmet, turban, songkok
insects	cockroach, beetle, mosquito, fly, wasp
languages	Arabic, Mandarin, Hindi, French, Spanish
liquors	whisky, brandy, gin, vodka, rum
meats	beef, mutton, chicken, pork, veal
metals	lead, silver, gold, iron, copper, bronze
occupations	doctor, artist, musician, priest, teacher
receptacles	box, carton, brief-case, purse, trunk,
relatives	aunt, uncle, niece, cousin, mother-in-law
roadways	road, highway, avenue, street, lane
seasons	summer, winter, autumn, spring
stationery	pencils, pens, ink, writing pads, envelopes, paper clips
spices	salt, pepper, garlic, sauce, mustard, curry powder
tools	hammer, spanner, screwdriver, plane, chisel
vehicles	car, bus, taxi, lorry, bicycle, train
weapons	pistols, rifles, shotguns, hand grenades

175

3. Receptacles: One word for many

A receptacle is a container for keeping things in or for holding.

1. Can you give a definition for the common receptacles listed below?

ashtray	cigarette-case	jug	safe
bag	clothes-basket	kettle	school-bag
barrel	coffee-pot	mail-bag	shopping basket
basin	cup	mug	suitcase
basket	cupboard	packet	tank
bath	desk	packing-case	teapot
bin	dish	pail	test-tube
bookcase	drawer	pan	thermos flask
bookshelf	dustbin	petrol tank	tiffin carrier
bottle	egg-cup	piggy bank	tin
bowl	envelope	pocket	travelling bag/case
box	filing cabinet	post-box	trunk
bucket	glass	pot	tub
can	handbag	purse	vase
carton	jar	refrigerator	wallet
case	jewel-case/box	sack	waste-paper basket

thermos flask

tiffin carrier

filing-cabinet

2. Below are the definitions of less well-known receptacles:

brief-case	a leather handbag for documents, papers, etc.
cabinet	a piece of furniture in which beautiful things are kept for show or display
chest	a large strong box with a lid for keeping personal belongings, etc. in
cistern	a water-tank in a building
compact (powder compact)	a small container of face-powder, usually carried in a woman's purse/handbag
crate	a box or framework made of wood for holding/transporting fruit, crockery, furniture, etc.
drum	a large cylindrical container for liquids, e.g. oil
flask	a bottle for carrying drinks
gas tank	a large round tank for storing gas, e.g. cooking gas

176

hamper	a large food basket with a cover
holster	a leather case for a pistol
knapsack	a leather or canvas bag carried by a hiker (or soldier) on his back
locker	a small cupboard with a lock for keeping clothes, books, etc. in
locket	a small metal case (usually heart-shaped) for holding a picture or a lock of hair of someone, worn around the neck on a chain
pouch	a small bag or purse carried in the pocket or on a belt
satchel	a bag for carrying school books
shrine	a place where sacred things are kept
till	a drawer for keeping money, as in a shop
urn	a vase for holding the ashes of a dead person
vat	a large tank or tub for liquids, e.g. dyes
vault	an underground room for valuables (money and jewellery) as in a bank
wardrobe	a piece of furniture for keeping clothes in

3. Because receptacles are containers they have the following measurements and parts:

1 corner
2 top
3 breadth
4 depth
5 edge
6 side
7 length
8 height
9 back
10 thickness
11 bottom
12 end
13 width

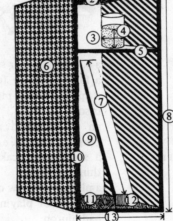

4. Places: One word for many

abattoir	a place where animals are butchered or slaughtered for market
aerodrome, airfield	a large field for aeroplanes
aquarium	a place where fishes and water plants are kept for public view

177

archives	a place where public records are kept
attic	a room just under the roof of a house
auditorium	a hall for lectures, concerts, etc.
aviary	a place where birds are kept
bar	a place where strong drinks (alcohol) are sold and served
bakery	a place where bread is baked and sold
brewery	a factory where beer is made or brewed
cabin	a room on a ship or aircraft

cabin

cafe	a coffee-house or small restaurant
cannery	a factory where food is processed and canned
canteen	a special eating place in a building where food is sold
cellar	an underground room for storing wine and other provisions, e.g. coal, firewood
confectionery	a shop where cakes, candies and other sweet things are sold
court	a place where law cases are heard
court	a place for playing certain games, e.g. tennis, badminton
crèche	a place where young children are looked after while their parents are at work
dairy	a place (usually in a farmhouse) where milk is made into butter and cheese
dispensary	a place where medicine is prepared

178

distillery	a place where alcoholic drinks (e.g. whisky, brandy) are made
deck	a wooden floor on a ship
depot	a place where buses are kept
dock	a place where ships are loaded, unloaded, repaired or built
dormitory	a large sleeping room with many beds, e.g. in a hostel
dump	1. a place for dumping rubbish (usually a public dumping ground)
	2. a place for storing military supplies, e.g. ammunition
emporium	a shop selling a large variety of goods
factory	a place where goods are manufactured
farm	a piece of land for growing vegetables, fruit or crops, or for raising animals, e.g. cattle and sheep
flat	a single floor of a building used as a home
foundry	a place where metal, glass, etc. is melted and moulded
gallery	a long room where works of art are exhibited
garage	a place where cars are kept or repaired
granary	a place where grain (e.g rice, wheat) is stored
greenhouse	a glass house usually kept at a warm temperature for growing delicate and rare plants
grocery	a grocer's shop; a place for selling household provisions
gymnasium	a hall with equipment for physical exercise
hall	a building or large room for meetings, games, concerts, exhibitions, etc.
hangar	a shed where aeroplanes are kept
harbour	a place of shelter for ships
hatchery	a place for artificial hatching, e.g. of turtle eggs
hospital	a large building where the sick and injured are treated and cared for
hostel	a building where students or nurses, etc. live
hotel	a building where rooms and meals are available for travellers
institution	a building used for education, or for cultural or charitable work
kindergarten	a school for very young (pre-school) children
kitchen	a room used for cooking

laboratory	a place for scientific experiments
laundry	a place where clothes are washed and ironed
mill	a factory with machinery for making cloth, paper, etc.
mine	a large hole dug in the earth to get minerals or precious stones
mint	a place where coins are made
mortuary	a place where dead bodies are kept before burial
mosque	a Muslim place of worship
museum	a building in which interesting, rare and old objects are displayed
night-club	a club open at night for entertainment
nursery	1. a child's playroom in a house
	2. a place where young children are looked after while their parents are at work
	3. a place where young trees and plants are grown
oasis	a fertile area in the desert

oasis

observatory	a building for observing the stars, planets, weather, etc.
office	a room for doing business or clerical work
orphanage	a home for orphans (children with no living parents)
pagoda	an Eastern temple with several storeys
pantry	a small room (usually adjoining a kitchen) where foodstuffs are stored
park	a large piece of land where people can relax
pier/jetty	a structure built out into the water as a landing-place for boats

180

porch	a covered entrance to a building
quarry	a place where stone, etc. is got out of the ground for use in building
reformatory	an institution where young law-breakers are sent to be trained as good citizens
reservoir	an artificial lake where water is stored for use by the public
restaurant	a place where people can get food and drink
ring	an enclosed space for a boxing match, wrestling, etc.
rink	a stretch of ice for skating
sawmill	a factory where logs are sawn by machinery into planks
shipyard	a place where ships are built or repaired
stadium	a place for outdoor or indoor games with seating all round
stall	a small place for selling things, e.g. at a market
studio	1. a place where a painter, sculptor or photographer works
	2. a place where films are produced, or a room where radio and television work is recorded
supermarket	a large shop where one serves oneself with food and goods
surgery	a place where doctors and dentists carry out their work
temple	a Hindu or Buddhist place of worship
theatre	a place where plays are acted or where films are shown
track	a specially prepared part of a field used for horse races, athletics events, etc.

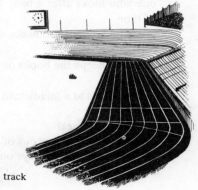

track

tuckshop	a shop where school children can buy food and drink
university	an institution of higher learning which gives degrees to graduates
vineyard	a piece of land on which grapes are grown
warehouse/godown	a building or shed for storing goods
ward	a section of a hospital where patients stay
wharf, quay	a place where ships come alongside for landing, loading, etc.

5. Occupations: One word for many

accountant	one who keeps accounts for a business
actor	one who plays a part on the stage or in a film
announcer	one who reads out information on radio or television, or at some public function

announcer

apprentice	one who is learning a trade
architect	one who designs buildings and sees that they are properly constructed
astrologer	one who tells the future from the stars
astronaut	one trained for space travel
astronomer	one who studies the moon, sun, planets, and stars
author	one who writes books and stories
baby-sitter	one who looks after a baby for a certain period of time
beautician	one who is trained to make women look beautiful
bookkeeper	one who keeps the books or accounts of a business
broker	one who acts as a middleman in buying and selling
butcher	one who sells meat
carpenter	one who makes things out of wood
cashier	one who receives and pays out money in a bank, shop or firm

182

chemist, pharmacist	one who prepares and sells medicines and health products
clerk	an office worker who writes letters, keeps minor accounts, does typing work, etc.
coach	one who gives special training in games and athletics
cobbler	one who mends shoes
contractor	one who makes an agreement (a contract) to supply goods, to do work, etc. at a fixed price
craftsman	a skilled workman
dentist	one who attends to people's teeth
designer	one who creates fashions or designs (e.g. clothes)
detective	one whose job is to catch criminals

detective

developer	one who improves an area by putting up houses, buildings, recreational facilities, etc.
draughtsman	one who draws plans for buildings
editor	one who improves and prepares a publication for printing
electrician	one who fits or repairs electrical devices
engineer	1. one who is in charge of machinery or engines (e.g. on a ship)
	2. one who builds roads, bridges, railways, etc.
fishmonger	one who sells fish
florist	one who sells flowers
goldsmith	one who makes and sells gold articles
grocer	one who sells foodstuffs and other household needs
greengrocer	one who sells fresh vegetables and fruit
hawker	one who moves from place to place to sell things
interpreter	one who translates orally words spoken in a foreign language

183

importer	one who brings in goods from foreign countries (the opposite of exporter)
jeweller	one who sells jewels and sets them
jockey	one who rides horses in races
journalist	one who writes, edits or publishes a newspaper
labourer	one who does unskilled manual work
laundryman	one who washes and irons clothes
lawyer	one who handles matters of law and fights court cases
locksmith	one who repairs and makes locks
magistrate	a judge in a lower court

magistrate

maid (servant), amah	a woman employed to do housework
mechanic	one who works a machine and usually knows how to repair it
midwife	a woman trained to help in childbirth
model	one who shows off fashions
musician	one who sings or plays a musical instrument for a living
newsagent	one who supplies newspapers, magazines, etc.
nurse	one who looks after sick people (usually in a hospital)
office-boy, peon	one who does odd jobs in an office
optician	one who tests eyesight and sells spectacles, lenses, etc.
pawnbroker	one who runs a pawnshop
physician	a doctor who treats diseases with medicines
pilot	one who guides a ship or flies an aeroplane
plumber	one who fits or repairs water-pipes, drains, sinks, toilets, etc.
porter	one who carries luggage at the airport, railway station, etc.
receptionist	one who receives callers, e.g. in an office, clinic, hotel

reporter	one who gathers news for a newspaper or magazine
retailer	one who sells goods in small quantities
salesman	one who sells goods in a shop, or to other shops, or from house to house
secretary	a trusted person who writes letters, keeps records, etc. for someone or for a company
spy	one who gets secret information, especially from an enemy country
stenographer	one who can do shorthand and typewriting
steward, stewardess/ hostess	one who serves and looks after passengers on an aeroplane or a ship
surgeon	a doctor who performs operations
surveyor	one who measures and maps out a piece of land
technician	a highly skilled scientific or industrial worker
telephone operator	a person who receives and directs telephone calls to the right persons

telephone operator

translator	one who re-writes from one language into another
undertaker	one who arranges funerals
usher, usherette	one who shows people to their seats in a cinema, theatre, auditorium, etc.
veterinarian	one who cures animals of diseases
waiter	a man who serves at tables in a restaurant
watchmaker	one who makes or repairs watches
watchman	one who guards a building, especially at night
warder	a guard in a prison
wholesaler	one who sells goods in large quantities

6. Types of Persons

accomplice	a person who helps one to do wrong
addict	one who is unable to free himself from a harmful habit, e.g. drugs
alien	one from a foreign country
amateur	one who takes part in an activity for the love of it and not to earn money
bachelor	an unmarried man
bankrupt	a person who is unable to pay his debts
busybody	one who meddles or interferes in the affairs of others
citizen	one who is a member of a particular country by birth or by naturalization
connoisseur	one who has a special skill in judging food, wines, etc.
conscript	one who is compelled by law to serve in the armed forces
consultant	one who gives specialist, professional advice to others
contemporary	a person born and living at the same time as another
criminal	one who commits a crime
customer	one who buys things at a shop
debtor	one who owes something (usually money) to another
donor	one who gives to others, e.g. money, goods
egoist	one who likes talking about himself and believes that he is more important than others
emigrant	one who leaves his own country to settle in another
employee	one who is employed (works for) another
employer	one who employs others to work for him
(eye) witness	a person who himself sees an event happen, e.g an accident
fiancé	a man to whom a woman is engaged to be married
fiancée	a woman to whom a man is engaged to be married
genius	one who is extremely intelligent
gossip	one who spreads idle talk about others
graduate	one who has successfully completed a course of study at a university or college

host	one who entertains others, especially at home
hypocrite	a person who says one thing and does another
immigrant	a person coming into a country from abroad to make his home there
kidnapper	a person who takes another away (usually by force) in order to demand money or something else for his safe return
miser	one who hoards money because he cannot bear to part with it
opponent	a person who takes the opposite side, especially in playing or fighting
optimist	one who looks on the bright side of life
orphan	a child whose parents are dead
patron	one who gives strong support (financial or otherwise) to some activity or organization
pessimist	one who looks on the dark side of things
philanthropist	a person who is kind and helpful to those who are poor or in trouble, especially by making generous gifts of money
pickpocket	one who steals from people's pockets
pilgrim	one who journeys to a holy place
recruit	a new member in an organization or in the armed forces
referee	a judge in charge of a team game, e.g. football
refugee	a person who has fled his country for political reasons or during a war
shoplifter	one who steals goods from a shop while pretending to be a customer
spectator	one who watches an event or sport without taking part
spinster	a woman who has never married
vegetarian	one who does not eat meat (or any animal flesh)
volunteer	one who offers his services for no pay
widow	a woman whose husband is dead
widower	a man whose wife is dead

7. Selected Groupings: One word for many
A. *Words pertaining to Business, Industry, etc.*

account (n)	a record of money owed, received or paid out over a certain period
advertisement (n)	a notice or announcement showing the good

	qualities of something to try to make people buy it
alloy (n)	a metal made by mixing together two or more different metals
career (n)	a job or profession for which one is trained and which one intends to remain in for life
cash (n)	money in coins and notes, rather than cheques
cheque (n)	a written note to a bank to pay a named amount of money
discount (n)	a reduction made in the cost when buying goods
economical (adj)	not wasteful; using money, time, goods, etc. carefully
exports (n)	goods made in one country for sale in another country
guarantee (n)	a written promise that something is what it is supposed to be, or that what someone has agreed to do, will be done
imports (n)	goods brought into the country from another country
insure (vb)	to make an arrangement so that a certain amount of money will be paid for loss of life, injury or damage to property
interest (n)	money paid for the use of money
invest (vb)	to put money into an organization with the hope of making more money
monopoly (n)	something of which one person or a group has complete unshared control to provide a service, trade in something, produce something, etc.
occupation (n)	a job; employment
profession (n)	an occupation requiring special training or education
quality (n)	a high degree of goodness (e.g. of goods)
salary (n)	fixed regular pay at definite times (e.g. weekly, monthly), especially for higher skilled workers and professionals
tariff (n)	a tax collected by the government on goods coming into (or going out of) a country
tax (n)	money paid to the government according to one's income, property, or goods bought
wages (n)	payment for labour or services according to the time taken or amount produced, paid weekly or daily (compare with salary)

Other useful words when talking or writing about business, finance, etc:

a balance	a deposit	commerce	an industry
a bargain	a fee	currency	an office
a bill	a gain	economics	an organization
change	an income	finance	dear/expensive (adj)
charge (vb)	a profit	trade	free (adj)
credit	a rate	a company	valuable (adj)
debt	a service	a firm	

an office

1 file	10 envelope	17 typewriter
2 operator	11 adding-	18 carbon-paper
3 switchboard	machine/calculator	19 notebook/
4 fan	12 diary	notepad
5 filing-cabinet	13 letter basket	20 calendar
6 telephone	14 desk	21 (hole-)punch
7 blotter/	15 waste-paper	22 stapler
blotting-pad	basket	23 staples
8 paper-clip	16 secretary/	
9 writing paper	typist	

B. *Words pertaining to Government and Administration*

abdicate (vb)	to give up an official position (especially that of king or queen)
administration (n)	the control or direction of affairs of a country

189

amendment (n)	a change made in, or suggested for, a law
bureaucracy (n)	government by officers who are appointed to run various state departments
capitalism (n)	a system where private individuals own and control wealth, production and trade with little controlled activity by the government
census (n)	an official count of a country's total population, etc.
communism (n)	a classless society and political system where the state or the people as a whole control production
compulsory (adj)	something one has to do because of a law or a rule
curfew (n)	a rule that all people should be indoors at a stated time
customs (n)	taxes paid on goods entering a country
demonstrate (vb)	to show strong feelings for or against something
democracy (n)	a form of government in which the people choose their leaders and in which there is freedom of speech, thought, etc.
duty (n)	what one must do because one thinks it is right
elect (vb)	to choose someone by voting
govern (vb)	to rule
independence (n)	freedom from another (usually another country's control)
justice (n)	the quality of moral rightness and fairness
law (n)	rules that are made by the government to guide the behaviour of the people in the society
majority (n)	the larger part or number of something
oppose (vb)	to speak, or act against something
opposition (n)	the political parties opposed to the government in power
overthrow (vb)	to defeat or remove a government by force
party (n)	a political group
politics (n)	the art or science of government
policy (n)	a plan of action taken by a group or organization to guide and determine decisions
represent (vb)	to act for or on behalf of others
revolt (vb)	to try to bring down a government, ruler, or authority by force
rights (n)	something which one may do or claim because of law

| statistics (n) | facts, figures, measurements, etc. collected for a particular purpose |
| unite (vb) | to join together and become one |

C. Words pertaining to Instruments, Machines, etc.

| apparatus | a set of instruments, materials, tools, machines, etc. needed for a particular purpose, e.g. laboratary apparatus |

1 balance/scales
2 pan
3 weights
4 meter
5 dial
6 needle/pointer
7 pestle
8 mortar
9 beaker
10 test-tube
11 flask
12 bunsen burner
13 tripod
14 rubber tubing
15 bench
16 stool
17 microscope
18 lens
19 slide
20 crystals
21 magnet
22 pipette

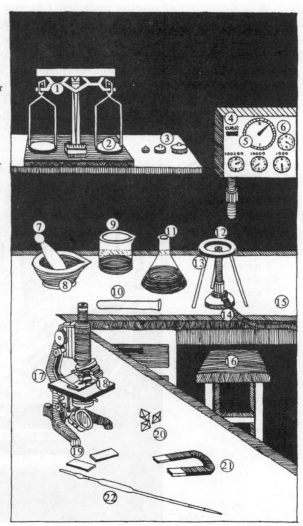

laboratory
apparatus

appliance	an instrument or device for use in the house, especially one using electricity, e.g. a vacuum cleaner
device	something which has been made for a special purpose, e.g. a mousetrap is a device for catching mice
equipment	all the different things needed to carry out a certain piece of work or for a certain purpose, e.g. office equipment (see page 189).
instrument	a mechanical device for some special purpose; an object used to help in work, e.g. medical instruments—forceps, scalpel, stethoscope
machine	an apparatus or man-made instrument with moving parts that can do work, e.g. a sewing machine
tool	an instrument used by a workman to do work (see diagram below)

1 spade
2 (garden) fork
3 shears
4 trowel
5 spanner
6 (work)bench
7 chopper
8 (pen-)knife
9 screwdriver
10 wrench
11 pincers
12 chisel
13 file
14 vice
15 sandpaper

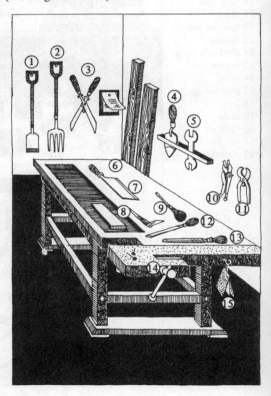

tools

D. *Words pertaining to Literature and Learning*

agenda	a list of the business or subjects to be considered at a meeting
album	a book (usually with blank pages) used for collecting stamps, photographs, drawings, etc.
autobiography	a record of one's life written by oneself
autograph	a person's own handwriting
bibliography	a list of all books, articles, etc. used in the preparation of a book or article, usually appearing at the end
biography	the history of the life of a person written by another
catalogue	a list of places, names, goods, etc. (usually with information about them), put in a special order so that they can be found easily
caption	a heading or words explaining a picture, drawing, etc.
copyright	the right in law to be the only producer, seller, or broadcaster of a book, film, play, etc.
dialogue	a conversation between two people
diary	a book containing a daily record of the events in a person's life
dictionary	a book that gives a list of words in alphabetical order with their meanings and pronunciations
directory	a book or list of names, facts, etc. usually in alphabetical order (e.g. a telephone directory)
encyclopaedia	a book or set of books dealing with every branch of knowledge
glossary	a list of explanations of words, especially unusual ones, at the end of a book
ledger	an account book recording the money gained and spent of a business, bank, etc.
memoirs	the story of the interesting and memorable experiences of one's own life
memorandum	a note to help one remember better
research	detailed study of a subject so as to learn new facts about it
review	an article giving a judgement on a new book, play, film, etc.
series	a set of successive, linked articles, stories, programmes, etc.

E. *Words pertaining to Medicine, Illness and Death*

ambulance (n)	a vehicle for carrying sick or injured people to hospital
amnesia (n)	loss of memory (either partly or completely)
amputate (vb)	to cut off parts of the body (especially the limbs) for medical reasons
anaesthetic (n)	a substance that produces an inability to feel pain; or allows someone to lose consciousness
antiseptic (n)	a substance which destroys germs—in order to stop flesh or blood from developing a disease
convalescence (n)	a period of time in which a person recovers from an illness
contagious (adj)	(of a disease) that can be easily spread from person to person by touch
diagnose (vb)	to be able to discover the nature of a disease by its symptoms (outward signs of an illness)
epidemic (n)	an infectious disease affecting many people at the same place and time
homicide (n)	the act of killing a human being
infectious (adj)	(of a disease) that can be spread by germs in the air
immune (adj)	free or protected from infection
obituary (n)	a notice (usually in the newspaper) that someone has died
post-mortem/ autopsy (n)	an examination of a dead body to find out the cause of death

Below are more useful words pertaining to the medical services:

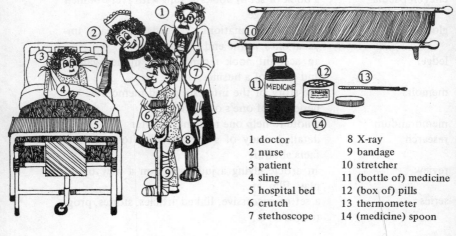

1 doctor
2 nurse
3 patient
4 sling
5 hospital bed
6 crutch
7 stethoscope
8 X-ray
9 bandage
10 stretcher
11 (bottle of) medicine
12 (box of) pills
13 thermometer
14 (medicine) spoon

quarantine (n)	confinement to one place for a period of time so that someone or something that may be carrying a disease, may not spread it
stethoscope (n)	an instrument used by doctors for listening to the action of the heart and lungs
suicide (n)	the act of killing oneself

F. *Words pertaining to Studies or Sciences*

anthropology	the scientific study of the nature of man (his body, his mind and his society)
archaeology	the study of the buried remains of ancient times, e.g. houses, pots, tools, weapons, etc.
astrology	the art of telling the future by the study of the stars
astronomy	the scientific study of the sun, moon, stars and other planets, etc.
biology	the scientific study of living things—plants and animals
botany	the scientific study of plants
geology	the study of the materials (rock, soil, etc.) which make up the earth
horticulture	the scientific growing of fruit, flowers, and vegetables
psychology	the study of the mind and the way it works, and of human behaviour
surveying	measuring, judging and recording on a map the details of an area of land
technology	the branch of knowledge dealing with practical scientific and industrial methods
zoology	the scientific study of different animals, where and how they live

G. *Words pertaining to War and the Armed Forces, etc.*

ambush (n)	a surprise attack on an enemy, from a hiding place
ammunition (n)	things fired from a weapon, e.g. bullets, bombs, explosives
aggression (n)	the starting of a quarrel, fight or war without real reason
casualties (n)	military people lost through death, wounds or illness

195

convoy (n)	a number of ships, army vehicles, etc. travelling together under escort for the sake of safety
diplomacy (n)	the art and practice of establishing and continuing relations between nations
espionage (n)	spying; the finding out of political secrets of countries to be passed on to their enemies
evacuate (vb)	to take all the people away from a place because of some danger
invade (vb)	to enter a country as an enemy so as to take control of it
manoeuvre (n)	the movement of troops or war ships so as to gain an advantage over an enemy
mobilize (vb)	to get soldiers, army vehicles, etc. ready for war
neutral (adj)	taking neither side in a dispute, war, etc.

Below are more useful words pertaining to the armed forces:

A ARMY
1 gun
2 guided missile
3 tank
4 soldier
5 jeep
6 bayonet
7 rifle
8 shell

9 (hand-)grenade
10 bullet/cartridge
11 machine-gun
12 pistol
13 revolver
14 trigger
15 barrel

B NAVY
16 warship
17 submarine
18 periscope
19 torpedo
20 aircraft-carrier

C AIR FORCE

21 bomber
22 bombs
23 fighter plane
24 cockpit

25 parachutes
26 navigator
27 pilot
28 control-panel

3 Derivations: Root Words, Prefixes and Suffixes

A great number of words in English are developed by combining word elements. For example, when new words are needed for new inventions, they are made up from **prefixes**, **word roots** and **suffixes**: **television** is **tele** (far), **vis** (sight), **ion** (condition or state of).

A **root** is a word in its simplest (and first) form. Most 'roots' come from Latin and Greek words, e.g. aqua (water).

A **prefix** is a word element added to the beginning of a root to form a new word, e.g. **dis**-agree.

A **suffix** is a word element added on the end of a root to form a new word, e.g. teach-**er**.

There are four good reasons why it is helpful to know and understand derivations:

1. By recognizing roots of word families, you can get the meaning of

197

a lot of new words. **Phon**, for example means sound, and it occurs in a large variety of words, all related to some aspect of sound, e.g. **telephone, phonetics, phonograph, phonology**.

2. Recognizing common prefixes and suffixes can also help you to grasp the meaning of a new word, especially if you can relate it to a familiar word. For instance, if you know what **credit** means, it is easy enough to work out **the changes in meaning** which different prefixes and suffixes convey in credit**or**, cred**ible**, **in**cred**ible**, and **dis**credit.

3. Furthermore, prefixes and suffixes can help you to build up new words with related meaning or of opposite meaning: e.g.

Using a prefix		**Using a suffix**	
produce	reproduce	any	anymore
wise	unwise	other	otherwise
university	pre-university	danger	dangerous

4. Prefixes and suffixes enable you also to form a word of a different word class (or part of speech) or of the same word class, given a particular word: e.g.

Forming nouns from adjectives			**Forming nouns from verbs**		
thick	—	thick**ness**	to agree	—	agree**ment**
active	—	activ**ity**	to invite	—	invit**ation**
anxious	—	anxi**ety**	to conclude	—	conclu**sion**
brave	—	brav**ery**	to defend	—	defen**ce**
difficult	—	difficul**ty**	to beg	—	beg**gar**
efficient	—	efficien**cy**	to type	—	typ**ist**
absent	—	absen**ce**	to criticize	—	critic**ism**

Forming adjectives from nouns			**Forming adjectives from verbs**		
danger	—	danger**ous**	to wash	—	wash**able**
friend	—	friend**ly**	to talk	—	talk**ative**
rock	—	rock**y**	to imagine	—	imagin**ary**
accident	—	accident**al**	to favour	—	favour**ite**
circle	—	circul**ar**	to satisfy	—	satis**factory**
law	—	law**ful**	to slip	—	slip**pery**
name	—	name**less**			
terror	—	terr**ible**			
metal	—	metal**lic**			
England	—	**English**			
expense	—	expens**ive**			
trouble	—	trouble**some**			

Forming verbs from nouns

courage	—	to encourage
circle	—	to encircle
friend	—	to befriend
prison	—	to imprison
memory	—	to memorize
class	—	to classify

Forming verbs from adjectives

rich	—	to enrich
large	—	to enlarge
fresh	—	to refresh
black	—	to blacken
loose	—	to loosen
modern	—	to modernize
simple	—	to simplify

Examples of Root Words

aqua (water)	aquatic, aqueduct
aud (hear)	audible, audience, audio
bio (life)	biology, bionic, biography
centum (a hundred)	cent, century, centimetre, centenary
dic (say)	dictate, dictator, verdict
duc (lead, draw)	education, produce, reduce
finis (end)	finish, final, infinite
graph (write)	graphics, autograph
liber (free)	liberty, liberation, liberal
mitt (send)	mission, missile, missionary
octo (eight)	octogan, octave, October
plus (more)	plus, plural, surplus
port (carry)	portable, porter, transport, export
primus (first)	prime minister, primary, primitive
scrib (write)	describe, script, manuscript
vis (see)	visible, vision, visual

Examples of Prefixes

a-	without	amoral, apathetic
ab-	away, from	abnormal, abstain, abstract
ac-, ad-, af-, ar-	toward	accident, advance, affix, arrive
ambi-	both	amphibian, amphibious, ambidextrous
ante-	before	antecedent, anteroom, anticipate
anti-	against	antiseptic, anti-aircraft, antidote
arch-	chief, leader	archbishop, arch-enemy
auto-	self	automobile, automatic, autobiography
bene-	good, well	beneficial, benefactor, benevolent
bi-, bis-	two, twice	bilingual, biennial, bisect
circum-	around	circumference, circumnavigate, circuit
co-, com-, con-	together, with	connect, cooperate, combine

contra-	against	contradict, contrary, contrast
de-	down, from	descend, depart, deflect, degenerate
dia-	through	diagonal, diameter
di-, dis-	apart from, not	different, disagree, disappear
ex-	out, out of, from	exclude, export, excommunicate
ex-	former	ex-policeman, ex-convict
fore-	before, in front of	foreground, foremost, foresee
hemi-	half	hemisphere
homo-	the same	homògeneous, homonym
hyper-	above, over, more than ordinary	hyperactive, hypersensitive, hypertension
in-, im-, il-, ir-	not	inconsiderate, impure, illegal, irregular
inter-	between	international, intermediate, intervene
mis-	wrong	misspell, mislead, mistake
ob-, op-, o-	against	object, obstruction, oppose
para-	beside	parallel, parable
peri-	around	perimeter
poly-	many	polygon, polygamist
post-	after	postpone, postscript, postmortem
pre-	before	prepare, precede, pre-war
pro-	forward, before	propose, progress, produce
re-	back, again	rejoin, rediscover, return
semi-	half	semicircle, semicolon
sub-	under	submarine, subway, subscribe
super-	above, over	superman, superhuman, super-lative
trans-	across	transport, transatlantic, transpose
tri-	three	tripod, triangle, triple, tricycle
ultra-	beyond	ultra-modern, ultra-violet
un-	not, without	unlikely, unpaid, unsafe, unknown
vice-	in place of, for	vice-president, vice-captain

Examples of Suffixes

-able, -ible	capable of being	portable, moveable, eatable
-ance, -ence	state of being	dependence, existence
-ant, -ent	one who	applicant, dependent, servant
-el, -et, -ette	little	cigarette, piglet, booklet

-er, -eer, -ier	one who	painter, engineer, financier
-ess	the female	actress, lioness, waitress
-ful	full of	thoughtful, thankful
-fy	to make, do	simplify, rectify, glorify
-icle, -sel	little	icicle, particle, morsel
-less	without	careless, hopeless, pointless
-ling	little	duckling, pigling, darling
-ment	state of being	enjoyment, merriment
-ory, -ary	a place for	factory, dormitory, library, dispensary
-ous	full of	famous, gaseous, glorious

4 Antonyms and Synonyms

An **antonym** is a word that is opposite in meaning to a given word. Antonyms can be formed in the following ways:
1. by adding a prefix to the given word
2. by changing the prefix of a given word
3. by changing the suffix of a given word
4. by a completely new word

Examples
1. By adding a prefix

able	—	**un**able	honest	—	**dis**honest
load	—	**un**load	obey	—	**dis**obey
accurate	—	**in**accurate	behave	—	**mis**behave
complete	—	**in**complete	understand	—	**mis**understand
possible	—	**im**possible	legal	—	**il**legal
patient	—	**im**patient	legible	—	**il**legible
regular	—	**ir**regular	smoker	—	**non**-smoker
responsible	—	**ir**responsible	citizen	—	**non**-citizen
climax	—	**anti**climax	curricular	—	**extra**curricular
clockwise	—	**anti**clockwise	ordinary	—	**extra**ordinary

2. By changing the prefix

absent	—	**present**	emigrant	—	**im**migrant
ascend	—	**descend**	encourage	—	**dis**courage
export	—	**import**	include	—	**exclude**

201

| external | — | internal | minimum | — | maximum |
| increase | — | decrease | pro-China | — | anti-China |

3. By changing the suffix

harmful	—	harmless	employer	—	employee
fearful	—	fearless	lively	—	lifeless
useful	—	useless	sensible	—	senseless
painful	—	painless			

4. By a completely new word
A. *Antonyms of Nouns*

amateur	—	professional	liquid	—	solid
adult	—	child	master	—	servant
arrival	—	departure	mountain	—	valley
back, rear	—	front	native	—	foreigner
birth	—	death	past	—	future
captivity	—	freedom	poverty	—	wealth
danger	—	safety	question	—	answer
entrance	—	exit	sale	—	purchase
friend	—	enemy	summer	—	winter
health	—	sickness	tenant	—	landlord
good	—	evil	victory	—	defeat
head	—	foot	war	—	peace
heat	—	cold	weakness	—	strength
host	—	guest	youth	—	age
income	—	expenditure			

B. *Antonyms of Adjectives*

ancient	—	modern	hollow	—	solid
angry	—	pleased	inferior	—	superior
beneficial	—	harmful	innocent	—	guilty
bright	—	dark	kind	—	cruel
calm	—	rough,	lazy	—	hard-working
		excited	modern	—	old-fashioned
common	—	rare	moving	—	stationary
cool	—	warm	neat	—	untidy
deep	—	shallow	negative	—	positive
delicate	—	strong	public	—	private
doubtful	—	certain	raw	—	cooked
fair	—	dark	safe	—	dangerous
fresh	—	stale	senior	—	junior
generous	—	selfish	sharp	—	blunt

202

tame	—	wild	unique	—	common
temporary	—	permanent	vacant	—	full
thrifty	—	extravagant	wasteful	—	economical
true	—	false, untrue	weak	—	strong

C.   Antonyms of Verbs

accept	—	refuse	give	—	take, receive
admit	—	deny	hit	—	miss
allow	—	forbid	join	—	separate
bend	—	straighten	lead	—	follow
blame	—	praise	love	—	hate
build	—	destroy	punish	—	reward
capture	—	release	push	—	pull
employ	—	dismiss	remember	—	forget
empty	—	fill	rise	—	fall
expand	—	contract	shorten	—	lengthen
fail	—	succeed	shout	—	whisper
float	—	sink	throw	—	catch
gain	—	lose	work	—	play

D.   Antonyms of Adverbs

alone	—	together	home	—	abroad
always	—	never	often	—	seldom
clearly	—	vaguely	regularly	—	occasionally
early	—	late	sometimes	—	never
everywhere	—	nowhere	wholly	—	partly
fast —		slowly	well	—	badly

A **synonym** is a word similar in meaning to another word. Below are some examples:

A.   Synonyms of Nouns

act	—	deed	cure	—	remedy
admission	—	entry	defect	—	fault
affection	—	love	desire	—	wish
beginning	—	start	display	—	exhibition
behaviour	—	conduct	donation	—	contribution
cause	—	reason	earnings	—	income
chance	—	opportunity	envy	—	jealousy
character	—	nature	evidence	—	proof
consequence	—	result	freedom	—	liberty
conversation	—	talk	grief	—	sorrow
competition	—	contest	harm	—	injury

hunger	— starvation	odour	— smell
idea	— thought	pleasure	— satisfaction
intention	— purpose	principle	— rule
journey	— trip	riches	— wealth
judgement	— verdict	strength	— power
knowledge	— learning	subject	— topic
midday	— noon	system	— method
misery	— unhappiness	value	— worth

B. *Synonyms of Adjectives*

accurate	— exact	fertile	— productive
alert	— watchful	frightened	— scared
annual	— yearly	furious	— angry
anxious	— worried	hard	— difficult
attractive	— pretty	hardworking	— industrious
awful	— terrible	ignorant	— stupid
brave	— courageous	jealous	— envious
bright	— intelligent	kind	— charitable
cautious	— careful	loyal	— faithful
clear	— distinct	mean	— stingy
clumsy	— awkward	necessary	— essential
coarse	— rough	normal	— usual
common	— ordinary	old	— elderly
confident	— hopeful	polite	— courteous
damp	— moist	safe	— secure
desperate	— hopeless	similar	— alike
diligent	— hard-working	strong	— powerful
		tired	— weary
doubtful	— uncertain	transparent	— clear
energetic	— active	wasteful	— extravagant
fair	— just		

C. *Synonyms of Verbs*

abandon	— leave	confess	— admit
aid	— help	control	— manage
allow	— let	cure	— heal
acquire	— get	decrease	— reduce
ask	— inquire	design	— plan
build	— construct	educate	— teach
buy	— purchase	find	— discover
capture	— seize	finish	— complete
choose	— select	forgive	— pardon

204

glance	–	look	reside	–	accept, take
hate	–	dislike	reveal	–	show
hurt	–	harm	search	–	seek
imagine	–	think	start	–	begin
increase	–	enlarge	surround	–	encircle
leave	–	depart	try	–	attempt
own	–	possess	vanish	–	disappear
protect	–	defend	want	–	need
receive	–	stay	watch	–	look

D. *Synonyms of Adverbs*

almost	–	nearly	generously	–	liberally
annually	–	yearly	gravely	–	seriously
certainly	–	surely	happily	–	joyfully
clearly	–	plainly	immediately	–	instantly
cleverly	–	skilfully	incorrectly	–	wrongly
completely	–	totally	intentionally	–	purposely
correctly	–	properly	powerfully	–	strongly
formerly	–	previously	rapidly	–	quickly
frankly	–	honestly	sincerely	–	truly
frequently	–	often			

5   Nationality Words: Names of Countries and People

The following lists give the names of some countries and continents and their corresponding adjectives and nouns. Note:

1. Adjectives to Describe Countries and People

These are formed in several ways:

1. ending in *-an*:   Australi*an* women, Germ*an* cars, Asi*an* food, Americ*an* industry
2. ending in *-ish*:   Engl*ish* weather, Dan*ish* butter, Span*ish* music, Finn*ish* furniture
3. ending in *-i*:   Israel*i* warfare, Pakistan*i* carpets
4. ending in *-ese*:   Vietnam*ese* refugees, Japan*ese* cars, Chin*ese* food, Portugu*ese* dances
5. other adjectives: Swiss, Greek, Arab/Arabian/Arabic, French, Dutch

2. Forming Specific and General Plural Nouns

When the plural is used to denote a certain or specific number of people it is formed in three ways:

A. *no change from the singular form:*

a Chinese	two Chinese
a Japanese	three Japanese
a Swiss	four Swiss
a Vietnamese	five Vietnamese

B. *by adding an -s:*

a German	two German*s*
an Indian	three Indian*s*
a Finn	four Finn*s*
a Spaniard	five Spaniard*s*

C. *by internal vowel change:*

an Englishman	two Englishm*en*
a Frenchman	three Frenchm*en*
a Dutchman	four Dutchm*en*
a Welshman	five Welshm*en*

Note that there are two specific plural forms for people from Scotland, i.e. Scots and Scotsmen.

When the plural is used to denote people in general, it is usually formed by adding **the** to the front of the specific plural form, although **the** is optional depending on the content of the sentence, e.g.

(The) Chinese are excellent ping-pong players.
The Swiss are famous for their watches.
(The) Pakistanis are well-known carpet makers.
(The) Australians are fond of playing sport.
(The) Russians excel in playing chess.

Note, however, that certain nationality nouns may take two forms of the plural when referring to people in general: e.g.

Englishmen
The English   } are very fond of cricket and tennis.

Frenchmen
The French   } enjoy a glass of wine with their meals.

206

Name of country or continent	Adjective	Nouns referring to a specific number		Plural nouns referring to people in general
		singular	plural (two +)	
China	Chinese	a Chinese	Chinese	(the) Chinese
Japan	Japanese	a Japanese	Japanese	(the) Japanese
Portugal	Portuguese	a Portuguese	Portuguese	(the) Portuguese
Vietnam	Vietnamese	a Vietnamese	Vietnamese	(the) Vietnamese
Arab Nations	{ Arab, Arabian, Arabic	an Arab	Arabs	(the) Arabs
Greece	Greek	a Greek	Greeks	(the) Greeks
Switzerland	Swiss	a Swiss	Swiss	(the) Swiss
Israel	Israeli	an Israeli	Israelis	(the) Israelis
Pakistan	Pakistani	a Pakistani	Pakistanis	(the) Pakistanis
Africa	African	an African	Africans	(the) Africans
America	American	an American	Americans	(the) Americans
Asia	Asian	an Asian	Asians	(the) Asians
Australia	Australian	an Australian	Australians	(the) Australians
Belgium	Belgian	a Belgian	Belgians	(the) Belgians
Brazil	Brazilian	a Brazilian	Brazilians	(the) Brazilians
Europe	European	a European	Europeans	(the) Europeans
Germany	German	a German	Germans	(the) Germans
Hungary	Hungarian	a Hungarian	Hungarians	(the) Hungarians
India	Indian	an Indian	Indians	(the) Indians
Italy	Italian	an Italian	Italians	(the) Italians
Malaysia	Malaysian	a Malaysian	Malaysians	(the) Malaysians
Norway	Norwegian	a Norwegian	Norwegians	(the) Norwegians
Denmark	Danish	a Dane	Danes	(the) Danes
Finland	Finnish	a Finn	Finns	(the) Finns
Poland	Polish	a Pole	Poles	(the) Poles
Spain	Spanish	a Spaniard	Spaniards	(the) Spaniards, (the) Spanish
Sweden	Swedish	a Swede	Swedes	(the) Swedes
Britain	British	{ *a Briton, a Britisher	{ Britons, Britishers	{ Britons, the British
England	English	an Englishman	Englishmen	{ Englishmen, the English
France	French	a Frenchman	Frenchmen	{ Frenchmen, the French

*The noun Briton is rarely used.

207

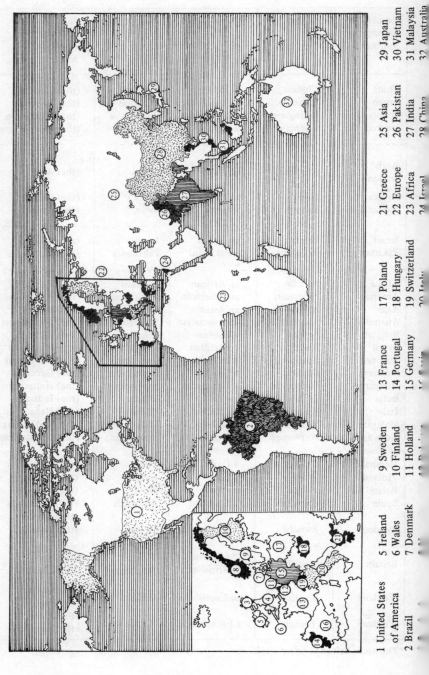

1 United States
  of America
2 Brazil

5 Ireland
6 Wales
7 Denmark

9 Sweden
10 Finland
11 Holland

13 France
14 Portugal
15 Germany

17 Poland
18 Hungary
19 Switzerland

21 Greece
22 Europe
23 Africa

25 Asia
26 Pakistan
27 India

29 Japan
30 Vietnam
31 Malaysia
32 Australia

208

Name of country or continent	Adjective	Nouns referring to a specific number		Plural nouns referring to people in general
		singular	plural (two +)	
Holland/The Netherlands	Dutch	a Dutchman	Dutchmen	{ Dutchmen { the Dutch
Ireland	Irish	an Irishman	Irishmen	{ Irishmen { the Irish
Scotland	{ Scots { Scottish	{ a Scotsman { a Scot	{ Scotsmen { Scots	{ Scotsmen { the Scots

6 Well-known Classical and Foreign Words and Phrases

Abbreviations used: (F) French
(L) Latin

ad hoc (L)	for this special object
à la carte (F)	choosing from a menu; opposite of a set meal
alma mater (L)	benign mother; the term is used by former students in referring to their university
au revoir (F)	goodbye; till we meet again
coup d'état (F)	a sudden decisive political move; an abuse of authority (e.g. when a group takes over the ruling power in a country)
de facto (L)	actually; in fact
en masse (F)	in a body; all together
en route (F)	on the way
erratum (L)	error
esprit de corps (F)	team-spirit
et cetera (etc.) (L)	and the rest
exit (L)	goes out
ex officio (L)	by virtue of his office
faux pas (F)	a false step; a mistake
ibidem (ibid) (L)	in the same place
impasse (F)	a dead-end; an insoluble difficulty
in memoriam (L)	to the memory of
in toto (L)	entirely
laissez faire (F)	policy of inaction; leaving things as they are

209

neé (F)	'born'; her maiden (unmarried) name being
nota bene (NB) (L)	note well
post mortem (L)	after death
répondez s'il vous plaît (RSVP) (F)	please reply
résumé (F)	a summary or abstract
status quo (L)	'the state in which'; the pre-existing state of affairs
subpoena (L)	under a penalty
tour de force (F)	a feat of strength or skill
verbatim (L)	word for word
versus (L)	against
via (L)	by way of
vice versa (L)	the other way round
vis-à-vis (F)	facing, opposite
voilà (F)	there! behold!

7 Abbreviations of National and International Organizations

AID (US) Agency for International Development

ASEAN Association of South East Asian Nations

BBC (GB) British Broadcasting Corporation

CD Corps Diplomatique (Diplomatic Service)

CIA (US) Central Intelligence Agency

CID (GB) Criminal Investigation Department

ECAFE Economic Commission for Asia and the Far East

EEC European Economic Community (the 'Common Market')

EFTA European Free Trade Association

FAO Food and Agriculture Organization of the United Nations

FBI (US) Federal Bureau of Investigation

GATT General Agreement on Tariffs and Trade

GPO (GB) General Post Office

IAEA International Atomic Energy Agency

IATA International Air Travel Association

IBRD International Bank for Reconstruction and Development (World Bank)

ICFTU International Confederation of Free Trade Unions

ICJ International Court of
    Justice
ILO International Labour
    Organization
IMF International Monetary
    Fund
NASA (US) National
    Aeronautics and Space
    Administration
NATO North Atlantic Treaty
    Organization
OPEC Organization of
    Petroleum Exporting
    Countries
NTUC National Trades Union
    Congress
SEATO South-East Asia Treaty
    Organization

UN United Nations
UNCTAD United Nations
    Conférence on Trade and
    Development
UNDP United Nations
    Development Programme
UNESCO United Nations
    Educational, Scientific and
    Cultural Organization
UNHCR United Nations High
    Commissioner for
    Refugees
UNICEF United Nations
    Children's Fund
WHO World Health
    Organization
YHA Youth Hostels
    Association

1. Miscellaneous abbreviations

a/c account
ad advertisement
AD *Anno Domini* (after the
    birth of Christ)
am before noon
approx approximately
asap as soon as possible
assoc associate; association
asst assistant
Av(e) Avenue
BA Bachelor of Arts (first
    university degree)
BC before Christ
Bro(s) brother(s)
BSc Bachelor of Science
    (first University degree)
C Centigrade
cc cubic centimetres
cert certificate; certified
Co Company

c/o care of; at the address of
Co-op Co-operative Society
cwt hundredweight
    (50. 8 kilograms)
Dept Department
Dip Diploma
Dip Ed Diploma of Education
DLitt Doctor of Literature
do ditto, the same
doz dozen
DPhil Doctor of Philosophy
Dr Doctor; debtor
DSc Doctor of Science
esp especially
Esq Esquire (in an address,
    appearing after the name
    without Mr)
F Fahrenheit
f foot, feet; female
fwd forward

211

GB Great Britain
GI (US) enlisted soldier
  (i.e. not an officer)
GMT Greenwich Mean Time
GNP Gross National Product
Govt Government
GP General Practioner
  (Medical Doctor, not a
  specialist)
h hour; height
HE His/Her Excellency
hp horsepower (of engines)
HQ Headquarters
hr(s) hour(s)
h/w herewith
IC identity card
in(s) inch(es)
Inc Incorporated
IOU I owe you
IQ Intelligence Quotient
Jnr Junior
JP Justice of the Peace
kg kilogram(s)
km kilometre(s)
KO knock-out
kph kilometres per hour
kw kilowatt(s)
l left; length; line
lb pound(s) (454 grams)
LLB Bachelor of Laws
LP long-playing (record)
LTD Limited
m male; married; metre(s);
  mile(s); million
MA Master of Arts (sec-
  ond university degree)
MB Bachelor of Medicine
MD Doctor of Medicine
mfr manufacturer
MP Member of Parliament
  (House of Commons);
  Military Police

mpg miles per gallon
mph miles per hour
Mr (either married or
  unmarried man)
Mrs (married woman)
Ms (either married or un-
  married woman)
ms(s) manuscript(s)
MSc Master of Science
  (second university degree)
NCO Non-Commissioned
  Officer
NE northeast
no(s) number(s)
nr near
NW northwest
op opus (work); operation
opp opposite
oz ounce(s) (28.35 grams)
pa per year
para(s) paragraph(s)
pd paid
PhD Doctor of Philosophy
PM Prime Minister
pm after noon; per month
PO (Box) Post Office (Box)
pp by the authority of;
  representing (before a name)
PR Public Relations
Pres President
pro professional
Prof Professor
QC Queen's Counsel (lawyer)
Rd Road
regd registered
Rep Republic; Representative
Rev(d) Reverend
RIP may he/they rest in
  peace
rpm revolutions per minute
RSVP please reply (on
  written invitations)

S South
sae stamped addressed
    envelope
s/c self-contained
Sch School
sci science
SE southeast
sec second
Sn(r) Senior
Soc Society
sp spelling; special
Sq Square
SS Steamship
St Saint; Street
STD direct dialling
    (by telephone)

SW southwest
T temperature
Tech Technical (College)
tel telephone
T. V. television
UFO unidentified flying
    object
Univ university
VHF very high frequency
VIP very important person
vs versus; against
W west
wc toilet
wpm words per minute
wt weight
yr year

2. Abbreviations used in Writing and Note-taking

ca about, approximately
cf compare with
ch(s) chapter(s)
cont continued
diff difference; different
eg for example
enc (l) enclosure; enclosed
et al and others
etc and all the rest
et seq and the following
excl excluding; exclusive
ff following
ibid in the same place
ie that is
incl including; inclusive
l(l) line(s)
loc cit in the place
    mentioned

misc miscellaneous
NB note well; take special
    note of
op cit in the work cited
    (mentioned)
p(p) page(s)
PS postscript
PTO please turn over
qv which may be referred to
    at another place
ref reference; refer to
resp respectively
sec section
v verse
viz namely; by name
vol volume

21. Rayfield, J. R., *Languages in a Bilingual Community*, p. 55.
22. Fredrick, *op. cit.*, p. 217.
23. *Ibid*, p. 219.

8 International Road Signs

1 Beware of animals
2 Children
3 Closed to pedestrians
4 Danger
5 Dangerous bend
6 Dangerous hill
7 Double bend
8 End of speed limit
9 Intersection
10 Level-crossing with gates
11 Level-crossing without gates
12 Merging traffic
13 No entry for all motor vehicles
14 No entry for all vehicles
15 No entry for pedal cyclists
16 No left (or right) turn
17 No U turns
18 Overtaking prohibited
19 Pedestrian crossing
20 Priority road ahead
21 Right (or left) bend
22 Road narrows
23 Road works
24 Roundabout ahead
25 Slippery road
26 Speed limit
27 Stop at intersection
28 Two-way traffic
29 Uneven road
30 Use of horn prohibited

PART

5

Units of Writing

1   Personal (friendly) Letters

1. The Layout of Personal Letters

Here are some reminders about the layout of personal (friendly) letters. The numbers refer to the numbered circles in the model letter on page 217.

(1) **Heading**. The heading consists of the street address, the city and state (and a postcode if there is one), and the date.

(2) In some countries the writer puts his name above his address but this is NOT the usual practice.

The writer's address is usually staggered—or indented—as the example shows. However, it may be written in the block form with each line beginning at the same place as the line above it. People who type their personal letters usually use the block form.

(3) Generally, a comma is put at the end of each line of the address and a full stop at the end.

(4) The date is written below the address with a space left between the address and the date. The date may be written in any of the following ways:

27 July 198–.	27th July, 198–.
July 27, 198–.	July 27th, 198–.
27/7/8–.	27.7.–.

(5) **Salutation**. The salutation of the letter varies depending on how well you know the person to whom you are writing. The safest way is to use **Dear** followed by the name by which you normally address the person. For example, if you usually address a person **James**, you begin **Dear James**. If you call him **Mr Lowe**, you begin **Dear Mr Lowe**. Increasing degrees of affection can be shown by

②

18 East Street,
①── Palmeston North, ── ③
New Zealand.

④─ 9th. August, 1980.

⑤
|
Dear Liza, ── ⑥

How are you? I hope everything is fine at home. I was sorry to hear of your father's illness, and I hope he is out of hospital by now.

I'm glad to say that I'm feeling fine and am settling down well to life in New Zealand. As you
⑦── can imagine I've been very busy and haven't had much time for writing letters.

Anyway, let me tell you a little bit about my New Zealand 'family' and the school I'm attending until I start university next year. Mr. and Mrs. Smith are my foster parents and they have two children, Jill and Peter. Jill is the same age as me and, in fact we're in the same sixth form class at Freyberg High School. As you can imagine, she is much bigger than I am but is very jolly and such great fun. Peter is only thirteen and is in form Ⅲ . They're both very good at sport and have introduced me to basketball and ice-skating. Mrs. Smith is a housewife but Mr. Smith is the Sales Manager of Hodder and Tolley, a large N.Z. firm. Mrs. Smith is an excellent cook and I've come to like roast lamb and roast beef with lots of vegetables. Of course, I've already put on some weight.

The lessons at Freyberg High School are most interesting. The teachers expect us to do a lot of work on our own in preparation for university life. As you know, I'll be entering Massey University next year where I'll be studying Veterinary Science. I hope that this course will enable me to help our farmers when I eventually return to Malaysia.

Please write and tell me what you've been doing. Give my best wishes to all my old school friends.

⑧── Yours sincerely,
⑨── Zaini

other expressions: **My dear Sue, Dearest Sue, My dearest Sue, Darling Sue.** Note however, that the first word and all nouns are capitalized.

(6) Note the comma after the salutation.

(7) **The body.** The body—or the main part of the letter—may begin below the comma of the salutation. Keep the paragraphs for easier reading.

(8) **Closing.** The closing also depends on how well you know the person to whom you are writing. To a member of the family or to a close friend you may like to use: **Your cousin, Your friend, Love, Best wishes, Fond regards, Yours affectionately,** etc. Remember though, that the safest form is **Yours sincerely.**

(9) **Signature.** This should always be hand written, never typed. Your first name or nickname is sufficient in letters to friends and relatives. The envelope should be written in the same indented style as the letter.

2. The Content of Personal Letters

Whatever the reason for writing friendly letters—to exchange news with a friend, to keep in touch with a relative—it usually includes **some** of the following points (many of which are concerned with health):

1. An enquiry about the health of the person to whom you are writing:

> How are you?
> How are you getting on?
> I hope you are feeling better?
> I hope that everything is fine with you.
> I hope that you have got over your cold.

2. An expression of concern about the health of a friend or a relative (known to both of you):

> How is your mother/father/sister, etc.?
> How is your father/mother now?
> I hope Mary/John/Mike, etc. is better now.
> I was sorry to hear of your mother's/father's/sister's, etc. illness/accident, etc.

3. A hope that he/she will soon be better:

> I hope that he/she will soon be better/well, make a speedy recovery, get over it, be out of hospital/bed, be up and about again.
> I hope your brother/sister, etc. is feeling better now.

218

4. An expression of relief that someone is well again:

> I am pleased/happy/glad to hear that your mother/sister, etc. is better now, has recovered, is all right again.

5. A brief statement about your own health:

> I am feeling fine.
> I am fine/well/quite well.
> I've had a bit of a cold lately.
> I'm sorry to say I've not been too well lately, I've had a temperature for the last few days, etc.

6. News (if any) about the health of a member of the family (who is known to the addressee):

> I'm afraid that my brother/father etc. is not very well, is having trouble with his back, etc., has broken his leg, etc., is in hospital with a . . ., may have to have an operation.

7. An enquiry for news about the person to whom you are writing:

> How are you getting on?
> How are things with you?
> How is life treating you?
> What have you been doing the last few weeks/months?
> I've been wondering how you are, how you're getting on.
> I haven't heard from you for some time.
> Do write and tell me what you've been doing.

8. The main body of the letter usually includes some news about yourself:

> A lot has been happening lately.
> I've been very busy lately.
> Life has been quite hectic lately, over the last few weeks.

OR

> Nothing much seems to have happened lately.
> Life has been very quiet in the last few weeks/months.
> I've been doing the same old things.

OR

> I must tell you about . . . .
> I wonder if you've heard about . . .?

219

Have you heard about . . .?
Did I tell you that . . .?
You will be surprised/pleased/interested to hear that . . . .

9. Passing on greetings from other people:

> My parents/sister, etc. send their best wishes.
> Kim and Kate send their regards.
> Joanne asked to be remembered to you.

10. A request that your greetings be passed on to someone:

> Please give your parents my best wishes/fond regards.
> Please remember me to your parents/sister/Jack.
> Wish your sister, etc. good luck in her examinations from me.
> Kind regards to . . . .

2 Formal Letters

These are letters written to a person whom you either do not know or do not know very well, for example, letters to newspapers, to people asking for references, etc. They are therefore similar to business letters although, unlike business letters, they may be hand written.

(1) **Heading**. Your address and the date are written in the top right corner as with personal letters. The block style (straight up and down) is usually preferred.

(2) **Inside address**. Unlike personal letters, the name, title and address of the person to whom you are writing is also given, usually at the head of the letter on the left.

(3) **Salutation**. If you know the name of the person to whom you are writing then you may use it in your salutation: **Dear Mr . . ., Dear Mrs . . ., Dear Miss . . . .** If you do not know the name of the addressee, begin **Dear Sir,** or **Dear Madam.** Note that the first letter of **Sir** is a capital.

(4) **Body of the letter**. This should be brief and to the point. Note that, unlike personal letters which generally start below the comma of the salutation, the body of the formal letter starts 3—5 spaces in from the margin. Each paragraph starts the same number of spaces in from the left margin.

99 Benthall Road,
London, N16.
28th August, 198–.

Miss A. G. Simms,
The Principal,
Benthall Road Primary School,
26 Benthall Road,
London.

Dear Miss Simms,

Shortly my family and I will be moving to a new house. During the preparations for our departure, I have come across a large number of pictures that I have kept over a period of ten years. The pictures have all been cut from magazines and newspapers and have been grouped according to subject.

As the house we are moving to is very small I will not have space to store this large collection of pictures and I was wondering if you and your teachers would be interested in having them in your school.

My son tells me that you have recently set up a special audio-visual room to accommodate the teaching materials in your school. I would be more than happy to donate my collection of pictures to your staff so that they can use them in their lessons.

Please let me know when it would be convenient for me to come and bring the pictures.

Yours sincerely,

JABray

(Mrs) J. A. Bray

(5) **Closing**. If you know the name of the addressee (e.g. Miss Brown), the correct close to use is **Yours sincerely** (note **sincerely** has a small s); if you do not know the name of the addressee, end the letter with **Yours faithfully**.

(6) The writer often prints or types his name beneath his signature since signatures are often difficult to read.

3 Business Letters

1. The Layout of Business Letters

Business letters usually involve writing either to or for a company. Their layout is much the same as for formal letters although there are some important additions.

(1) **Heading** (Printed Letter-head or Private Address).

If you are writing on behalf of a company, you will use paper with a **printed letter-head**. This letter-head includes the name, address, telephone number of the company (or sender), and may contain a description of the business, trade-mark, telegraphic address, telex, etc.

If you are writing a business letter as a private individual, your address will go, as usual, in the top right hand corner. As a business letter should be typed, the block style is most appropriate.

(2) **Reference**. Give a reference number if you have one. This is usually in the top left corner of the letter and may look like any of these:

Ref: No 352/6/b		Our ref: 352/6/b
Ref: 352/6/b	OR	Your ref: 482.23 Del.
Our ref: 352/6/b		

Sometimes a company may not use a filing number but instead give the initials of the person who dictated the letter, in capitals, and the initials of the secretary or typist, in small letters: NAY/rsk.

(3) **The Inside Address** and (4) **Salutation**. Unlike the friendly letter, a business letter requires an inside address above the body of the letter to the left. This consists of the full title and address of the person to whom you are writing. If you know the name of the person, you should put his name at the beginning of the address and then begin the letter **Dear Mr . . .**, **Dear Mrs . . .**, **Dear Miss/Ms . . .**:

Mr P. James,
64, Long Avenue,
Singapore.

Dear Mr James,

If you do not use the name of the addressee, and use the title only,
e.g. **The Manager**, **The Controller of Programmes**, etc., your letter
should begin **Dear Sir**, or **Dear Madam**:

Sales Recruitment and Training Manager,
W. & T. Avery Limited,
21, Conduit Street,
London, W. 1.

Dear Sir,

If you are not writing to any particular person in the firm, you
should begin **Dear Sirs**:

Museum of Science and Industry,
Jackson Park,
Chicago,
Illinois 60637.

Dear Sirs,

5. **Subject line.** It is helpful to give your letter a heading, stating the
subject. This comes **after** the salutation and is usually underlined.

6. **Body of the letter.** A business letter may be written in semi-block
(where the addresses are block but the paragraphs are indented),
or fully block (where no paragraphs are indented, and all parts of
the letter begin at the left margin). If you are writing for a company, generally you need to follow the style of the company's
letters.

7. **Closing.** When a letter begins **Dear Sir(s)** or **Dear Madam**, the ending is usually **Yours faithfully**. When a letter begins with the name
of the addressee (**Dear Mr James**), the ending is usually **Yours
sincerely**.

8. **Signature.** This is hand written and then followed by the writer's
position or status in the company. A woman may indicate her
marital status so that the person replying knows how to address
her, e.g. N. A. Nesbit (Mrs), S. J. Swift (Miss).

9. **Enclosure.** When something is enclosed with a letter, it is usual to
indicate this by the abbreviation **enc.** at the bottom left side of the
letter.

① — **EAGLEPRESS**

01-337 6334 · 08926-63958

43 aragon road morden surrey sm4 4qg england

Your ref: MR/kg — ②
Our ref: BM/gc

20th September, 198—.

The Director,
The Rubber Research Institute,
Ampang Road,　　　　　　——— ③
Kuala Lumpur.

Dear Sir, ——— ④

⑤ ——　A Malaysian rubber correspondent

Our publishing group runs two magazines covering
the rubber industry worldwide. We need a correspondent in Malaysia to send us about 1,000 words — ⑥
a month on anything to do with the Malaysian rubber industry. We are prepared to pay anything between £35 and £40 a month for this.

We would appreciate it if you could suggest someone in Malaysia who would be able to help us in
any way. The desired person needs to be actively
involved in the rubber industry and would need to
have a sound knowledge of production and sales
trends.

We have pleasure in enclosing the most recent edi-
tion of 'The Rubber Report'.

⑦ ——— Yours faithfully,

⑧ —— *BMackie*

B. Mackie,
Chief Editor.

Enc. ——— ⑨
c.c. Marketing Manager ——— ⑩